7

SOUL
MURDER

SOUL MURDER

PERSECUTION IN THE FAMILY

MORTON SCHATZMAN

 RANDOM HOUSE NEW YORK

WITHDRAWN

ACKNOWLEDGMENTS

Thanks are due to Drs. Ida Macalpine and Richard A. Hunter, editors and translators, and to Dawsons of Pall Mall, publishers, for permission to quote from Schreber's *Memoirs of my Nervous Illness;* to Sigmund Freud Copyrights Ltd., The Hogarth Press Ltd., and The Institute of Psycho-Analysis for permission to quote from *Analysis of a Phobia in a Five Year Old Boy*, Vol. X, and from *Psycho-Analytic Notes on an Autobiographical Account of a Case of Paranoia (Dementia Paranoides)*, Vol. XII, by Sigmund Freud, from *The Complete Psychological Works of Sigmund Freud* (also available in the *Collected Papers* of Sigmund Freud, published by Basic Books, Inc.); and to George, Allen & Unwin Ltd. and Basic Books, Inc., for permission to quote from *The Interpretation of Dreams* by Sigmund Freud.

We are publishing the photographs of Daniel Paul Schreber and Daniel Gottlieb Moritz Schreber by courtesy of Dr. Franz Baumeyer, who obtained them from his circle of acquaintances and from Daniel Paul's foster-daughter.

Library of Congress Cataloging in Publication Data
Schatzman, Morton.
Soul murder.
Bibliography: p.
1. Schizophrenia. 2. Family. 3. Schreber, Daniel Gottlieb Moritz, 1808-1861. 4. Schreber, Daniel Paul, 1842-1911. Denkwürdigkeiten eines Nervenkranken.
I. Title.
RC514.S318 616.8'982'071 72-6559
ISBN 0-394-48148-8

Manufactured in the United States of America
First Edition

Wer über gewisse Dinge den Verstand nicht verliert, der hat keinen zu verlieren. (He who does not lose his mind over certain things has no mind to lose.)

Gotthold Ephraim Lessing in his play
Emilia Galotti (1772): IV, vii.

CONTENTS

CONTENTS

PREFACE

Daniel Paul Schreber (1842–1911), an eminent German judge, went mad at forty-two, recovered, and eight and a half years later went mad again. It is uncertain if he ever was fully sane, in the ordinary social sense, again. Psychiatrists and psychoanalysts consider him a classic case of paranoia and schizophrenia. His father, Daniel Gottlieb Moritz Schreber (1808–1861), who supervised his upbringing, was a leading German physician and pedagogue. The father's influence was large in his time and after he died. The father thought his age was morally "soft" and "decayed" owing mainly to laxity in educating and disciplining children at home and school. He proposed to "battle" the "weakness" of his era with an elaborate system of child-rearing aimed at making children obedient and subject to adults. He expected his precepts, if followed, would lead to a better society and "race." He applied the same basic principles of training children as have totalitarian regimes, secular and religious. Like them he thought a child's obedience and discipline to be more important than anything else. He sired two sons; Daniel Gustav, the elder, went mad too and killed himself.

It would be of value to know if parents and societies that adopt obedience and discipline as preeminent goals of child education are more, less, or equally likely to drive children crazy than other parents and societies.

The views on family life of Dr. Schreber, the father, mirror, as if in caricature, ideologies widely held in the "liberal" West today: adult males must be dominant; sexuality in children and adolescents must be subdued; two adults (parents), however ignorant, bigoted, or intolerant they might be, must oversee their offsprings' morals until mid- to late adolescence; and children must learn early to submit, often uncritically, to their parents' wills.

In recent years we have become more aware of battered babies, neglected children, and maltreated children. But there are types of brutality more subtle and less dramatic that go on in many families. It is with these types and their long-lasting effects upon children that I deal here and in some of my daily work.

In this book I link the strange experiences of Daniel Paul Schreber, for which he was thought mad, to his father's child-rearing practices. I bring forth and match two sets of facts—the son's bizarre experiences as an adult and his father's techniques of educating children—and I conjecture about how they may be connected.

Regard the father's methods of raising children as one set of elements and his son's peculiar experiences as another set. I wish to define the operations by which the father's methods are *transformed* into elements of the son's experience. If an odd experience of the son seems recognizably related to a procedure of his father, I call the experience an *image* or a *transform* (i.e., the product of a transformation) of that procedure; I use the terms "image" and "transform" interchangeably.

Not all the son's experiences are images of his father's practices. Judge Schreber also had a mother, a grandmother who died when he was four and a half (Niederland, 1963), an older brother, three sisters, and nurses. His relation to each of them, theirs to each other, each's relation to each other's to him, his relation to each's relations to each other, etc., also likely appeared, transmuted, in his "nervous illness." But I can only point to this as possible, since little is known about most members of his family of origin and nothing, reliably, about the scenes they enacted together. Nor can I find images in the son's set of experiences for all elements in the father's set of child-rearing methods. The son's writing, like all writing, is a drastically abridged version of his experiences; he must have omitted many events in the years of his life he recounts there. Also, his mind may have transformed his experience of some of his father's activities so much that if he reported it, I cannot recognize it. My concern here is mainly with experiences of the son that I can show to be images of his father's conduct and with conduct of the father for which I can find images in the son's experiences.

I focus not on why, but on *how* Judge Schreber came to feel persecuted; not on what caused his feelings, but on events which can be correlated with them.

I propose that experiences he thought were supernatural revelations and doctors have seen as symptoms of mental illness can be regarded as *transforms* of his father's treatment of him. I also suggest his father had taught him as a child patterns of operating upon his experience such that later on he felt forbidden (or forbade himself) to see that his strange relation to God was a reexperience of his childhood relation to his father. This book illustrates and embodies this thesis.

My main focus here is on two minds, a father's and a son's, and on relations between them. My findings touch on many domains: child-rearing, education, psychiatry, psychoanalysis, psychology, religion, sociology, and others. In the last chapter I consider possible links between the father's views on raising children and the rise of Nazism; in the epilogue I look at likenesses among his views, those of the Russians today, and those of B. F. Skinner, the American behavioral psychologist.

I can only allude to other issues, given our state of ignorance. Certain individuals seen as mad seem to learn strange patterns of experience and behavior early in life. Much of what is seen as insanity can be considered a sort of adaptation to certain learning situations, however *mal*adapted it may be in the world outside those situations. Recent studies of the families of origin of people labeled schizophrenic reveal that odd experiences and actions of some schizophrenics can be rendered intelligible as responses to maddening families. How can we render intelligible the experience and conduct of *other* members of those families? In what situations did *they* learn to experience and act upon each other in the disturbing ways they do? In what sorts of social worlds do families with mad offspring live? I do not know the answers; in order to unveil them we may need to criticize *all* our patterns of child-rearing, education, and family life more radically than anyone yet has.

This book owes a lot to sources not discussed much in the text, especially to the published work on schizophrenia of Gregory Bateson and his colleagues and to discussions prior to my writing the book with David E. Schecter and R. D. Laing. A list of all the people who have influenced the ideas and shape of this book would be almost coextensive with a list of my colleagues and friends. Among those who have read parts of or all the text I wish to thank for their helpful suggestions in particular Mr. Robert Adkinson, Dr. Joseph and Mrs. Roberta Elzey Berke, Dr. Everett Dulitt, Dr. Aaron Esterson, Dr. Jean Houston, Dr. Murray and Mrs. Ellie Korngold, Mr. R. E. L. Masters, Dr. Doris Nagel, Dr. Fred and Mrs. Joel Sander, Dr. Thomas Scheff, Dr. Alan Tyson, and Dr. Harry Wiener. I am also grateful to Miss Vicky Rippere for finding certain references and helping in the work of translating passages from the German.

Parts of this book were published previously as an article (Schatzman, 1971) in *Family Process*.

SOUL
MURDER

Daniel Paul Schreber, the son

Daniel Gottlieb Moritz Schreber, the father

MODELS
OF MADNESS

Until recently investigators had studied individuals seen as schizophrenic, not their social contexts. The focus had been upon the "patients," not the behavior of other people toward them; it still is in certain circles. As a result, the concept of schizophrenia has been built upon only some of, not all, the data I think are needed to understand experiences of people considered schizophrenic.

Some persons regarded as schizophrenic whom I have known seemed to describe during their "illness," with symbols, their social situations, past and present. The more I learned of their lives the more truth I could see in what they were saying. Their families, however, would dismiss their words as signs or symptoms of illness and therefore invalid. Their doctors, unfamiliar with the social world in which the "illness" occurred, would too. The idea that someone is mentally ill makes it easy to call what he says invalid.

In this book I shall illustrate how one man, viewed as schizophrenic, alluded to some painful truths, while thought mad, about his childhood experiences. Neither some leading physicians of this century who labeled him mentally ill, nor anyone he knew, grasped the meaning of his message.

Daniel Paul Schreber began a career as a mental patient at forty-two, spent thirteen of his next twenty-seven years in mental asylums, and died there. At sixty-one he published *Memoirs of My Nervous Illness,* a book he compiled from notes about his experiences and thoughts while "suffering from a nervous illness." Although he started the work in a mental asylum with no idea of publishing, he changed his mind as he progressed with it. He came to think that "observations of my personal fate during my lifetime would be of value both for science and the knowledge of religious truth." Ida Macalpine and Richard Hunter, historians of psychiatry, who translated (1955) Schreber's *Memoirs* into English, say "Schreber is now the most frequently quoted patient in psychiatry" (p. 8).

Schreber ascribed his first two 'nervous illnesses" to "mental overstrain." The first, while he was chairman of a county court, was "occasioned," he said, "by my candidature for parliament" (the *Reichstag*); he lost the election (Niederland, 1963) and six weeks later entered a clinic as an inpatient where he stayed six months. He writes:

> After recovering . . . I spent eight years with my wife, on the whole quite happy ones, rich also in outward honours and marred only from time to time by the repeated disappointment of our hope of being blessed with children. (*Memoirs,* p. 63)

Then, a few weeks after taking up "the heavy burden" as president of the senate of the supreme court in Saxony (*ibid.,* pp. 61–62), "an extraordinary event occurred."

> During several nights when I could not get to sleep, a recurrent crackling noise in the wall of our bedroom became noticeable . . . ; time and again it woke me as I was about to go to sleep. Naturally we thought of a mouse. . . . But having heard similar noises innumerable times since then, and still hearing them around me every day in daytime and at night, I have come to recognize them as undoubted *divine miracles—*. (p. 64. Italics here and in all the passages I quote in this book are mine except where specified otherwise.)

4

A month later he entered the clinic again; he was fifty-one. He remained in asylums this time for nine years. Most of the events he describes in the *Memoirs,* published a year after his discharge, occurred during this long second episode; my book is concerned with these. We know much less about his last, four-year stay in a mental hospital, which ended with his death.

All the doctors who treated Schreber or have written about him have seen him as mentally ill. Schreber had a different view. He begins the introduction to his *Memoirs:*

> I have decided to apply for my release from the Asylum in the near future in order to live once again among civilised people and at home with my wife. It is therefore necessary to give those persons who will then constitute the circle of my acquaintance, an approximate idea at least of my *religious conceptions,* so that they may have some understanding of the necessity which forces me to various oddities of behaviour, even if they do not fully understand these apparent oddities.
>
> This is the purpose of this manuscript; in it I shall try to give an at least partly comprehensible exposition of *supernatural matters, knowledge of which has been revealed to me.* . . . I cannot of course count upon being fully understood because things are dealt with which cannot be expressed in human language; they exceed human understanding. . . . One thing I am certain of, namely that *I have come infinitely closer to the truth than human beings who have not received divine revelation.* (p. 41)

Later he writes:

> . . . I would count it a great triumph for my dialectical dexterity if through the present essay, which seems to be growing to the size of a scientific work, I should achieve only the one result, to make the physicians shake their heads in doubt as to whether after all there was some truth in my so-called delusions and hallucinations. (p. 123*n*)

He had experienced God for the first time at fifty-one during what he called his holy time; others had seen this period as the

5

acute phase of a psychosis. He was in daily contact with supernatural powers for the next eight years and possibly until he died at sixty-eight. When he speaks of his "nervous illness" he does not mean a neurotic illness, as the term is now used, or a mental illness, or any illness in the usual medical or psychiatric sense. In his "nervous illness" his "nerves" would attain "a state of high-grade excitation" and would "attract the nerves [or rays] of God" (p. 48). Generally, he regarded these experiences as "morbid" and unpleasant. While his "nerves" were in contact with God's "rays" he would gain knowledge of "supernatural matters." What he thought were divine revelations his doctors saw as delusions, as doctors today would.

Dr. Weber, one of Schreber's hospital doctors, in a report on him says his religious experiences give an idea of his "pathologically altered conception of the world" (Postscript to *Memoirs*, p. 273). Weber thinks a "mental illness" is "doubtless present" (*ibid.*, p. 275).

In reply Schreber writes:

> I deny absolutely that I am mentally ill or ever have been. . . .
> The medical expert's report . . . contains, in having accepted the presence in my case of paranoia (insanity), a blow in the face of truth, which could hardly be worse. (p. 286)

He says that during most of his time in the hospital Weber

> only became acquainted with the pathological shell, as I would like to call it, which concealed my true spiritual life. (p. 297)

A person in the modern era who has certain extraordinary experiences often finds himself in trouble. Usually, no one he knows has had similar experiences. No one accepts his testimony. Even if other people wanted to learn to experience the world as he does, which they generally do not, they would not know how to. And he would not know how to teach them to. If he persists in his strange experiences and in reporting them, they will likely see him as mentally ill.

The belief that mental illness of some sort causes certain unusual experience and behavior is extensive and strong. Official opinion nearly world-wide regards the bizarre experience and behavior of certain persons as occasioned by the mental illness called schizophrenia. Before the modern era official opinion thought much of the same experience and behavior to be of supernatural origin. Some persons who think so today are labeled schizophrenic for thinking it.

Much of Schreber's thinking while he was seen as ill was normal. Three years before Schreber was discharged from a nine-year stay in hospital, Dr. Weber writes:

> . . . Schreber now appears neither confused, nor physically inhibited, nor markedly affected in his intelligence . . . : he is circumspect, his memory excellent, he commands a great deal of knowledge, not only in matters of law but in many other fields, and is able to reproduce it in an orderly manner. He is interested in political, scientific and artistic events, etc., and occupies himself with them continuously. . . . (Postscript to *Memoirs*, p. 271)

An autopsy report (Baumeyer, 1956) mentions no cerebral damage.

Some of Schreber's experience, in his madness, resembles reported experiences of shamans or medicine men, i.e., specialists in ecstasy and the sacred in "archaic" cultures (see Eliade, 1960 and 1964). Like them he is "chosen" by supernatural powers; the sacred manifests itself through his sharpened senses; and he learns the names and functions of souls and higher beings, the language of birds, and a secret language—in his case, the "basic language [*Grundsprache*]" of God. He experiences visions and trances and sees, hears, and feels events hidden from other men. He says he is called, in "soul language,"

> "the seer of spirits," that is, a man who sees and is in communication with, spirits or departed souls. (*Memoirs*, p. 88)

Like some shamans, Schreber experiences an increase in light around him, wears women's clothes, and feels himself to be

7

bisexual. Like nearly all shamans, especially during their initiation, he endures bodily torture and dismemberment.

I think some experiences of many people labeled schizophrenic resemble those of shamans. People widely separated in space, language, culture, and prior spiritual beliefs have had strikingly similar experiences. Could anyone have them? More study is needed here, not only to learn more about "them," the shamans and schizophrenics, but about parts of our minds of which we may be usually unaware.*

Other cultures, especially those which honor shamans, and possibly even Schreber's own several hundred years earlier, might have regarded as valid experiences and inferences for which he was considered crazy. His accounts of his revelations and his arguments about God did not persuade his contemporaries, partly because they were committed to a different paradigm—mental illness—by which they construed his experiences. Psychiatrists then, as they would now, explained and dealt with their experiences of his strangeness with a well-articulated vocabulary, theory, and set of practices based upon the model of an illness inside him.

Schreber is considered a textbook case of paranoia and schizophrenia; both are mental illnesses. Eugen Bleuler (1950), who invented the term "schizophrenia" and developed the concept, thought Schreber was paranoid, schizophrenic, hallucinated, deluded, dissociated, autistic, and ambivalent. Bleuler saw Schreber's report of his experiences, like the words of mental patients generally, as material or productions, as semantic discharges of a disease process. He classified Schreber's statements and remarked upon their form and content, but did not try to under-

---

* Most of us in the presence of a man who experiences the extraordinary adopt the position of Hamlet's mother when Hamlet asks if she does not see the ghost:

HAMLET. Do you see nothing there?
QUEEN. Nothing at all; yet all that is I see.
How, I wonder, did she know she saw "all that is"?

8

stand them as valid messages. He said flatly about people he called paranoid:

> No dependence can be placed on the statements of the patients themselves. . . . (1924, p. 525)

Schreber's doctors adopted a similar posture toward him, as many would today.

Bleuler, like Emil Kraepelin before him, upon whose concepts Bleuler based many of his ideas about schizophrenia, was not interested in the upbringing of his patients. Kraepelin (1904), in his lecture "Paranoia, or Progressive Systematized Insanity," gives a long, detailed case history of a man, but never mentions his childhood, adolescence, or any member of his family of origin, and never mentions that he never mentions them.

Freud, unlike his predecessors, tried to understand what patients were saying and to link their experiences with events in their childhoods. In so doing he introduced the minds of people now called schizophrenic into the concept of the disease that supposedly afflicts them. Freud never met Schreber, but he wrote an analysis of him based upon the *Memoirs*. His study of Schreber is a pivotal statement of the psychoanalytic theory of psychosis and has had much influence. It is the origin of the view, held by most psychoanalysts, that paranoia arises as a "defense" against homosexual love, i.e., that the paranoid person is persecuted by his or her unconscious love, specifically for his or her parent of the same sex, which he or she experiences consciously as persecution from outside.

Psychoanalysts since Freud have been interested in their patients' childhoods. They have derived their data mainly from what their patients have told them. Since patients, like everyone else, never report their experiences entirely or precisely, this information cannot be complete and can be misleading. Theories built upon limited data often need revision when new facts come to light.

Freud's analysis of Schreber is unique among his case studies, since a source of "raw" data about Schreber's childhood, which Freud did not use, still exists. Schreber's father, a physician, orthopedist, and pedagogue, wrote eighteen books and booklets; many are about his methods of educating children; he applied them to his own children. Although Freud knew of Schreber's father, he did not use his writings as data, even though the father's books had been widely read and are still available. Bleuler had not even mentioned Schreber's father. Those who wrote about Schreber for the next fifty years did not use Schreber's father's writings as data either. Most did not turn to the *Memoirs;* they discussed only the passages that Freud had already quoted.

Thirteen years ago William Niederland (1959a), an American psychoanalyst, pointed out some striking likenesses between some of Schreber's odd thoughts and his father's techniques of bringing up children. I use several of Niederland's examples in the next chapters. Niederland has been researching Schreber's ancestry, upbringing, and adult life for over twenty years and has turned up valuable facts. He tries to show that his findings confirm Freud's conclusions about why Schreber became paranoid; he does not see that his findings call for radically new hypotheses.

I have read some of the father's writings, and have found
that several of Schreber's peculiar experiences, for which he was labeled paranoid, schizophrenic, insane, etc., can be linked to specific procedures of his father;
that the father's child-rearing practices could confuse any child;
and that he would have forbidden a child to see how confusing his methods were.

My study is an attempt to connect the mind of an adult, considered mad, to his father's behavior toward him as a child. We can never be sure of what actually has happened between a parent and child. This would be so even were we there to see it, since we could experience each's behavior toward the other, but not each's experience of the other. All reports of what has occurred between a parent and child are based to some extent upon the author's reconstructions. This is true, but less so, with autobiographies.

I am concerned here not with isolated traumatic events that may have happened once or twice in Schreber's childhood, but with *patterns* of events that happened *recurrently* and that can be linked with patterns of events he experienced repeatedly during his "nervous illness."

Although I confine myself to the study of Schreber's mind and his father's behavior, my findings, and how I construe them, may help in understanding others seen as paranoid or schizophrenic. What I have found brings other issues into view. Irony is everywhere. An eminent pedagogue has a psychotic son; it does not hurt his reputation. Freud, an avid reader, neglects—as do his followers—books on child-rearing by a man whose son's childhood experiences Freud is trying to derive. German parents rear their children by the ideas of a man whom many people now would see as sadistic or mentally ill.

We become aware of a gap in existing scholarship: no one has systematically searched for links between the separate reality seen by shamans, sorcerers, schizophrenics, and the divinely mad, and events in their childhoods. They all seem to dress their religious revelations in the social forms they have been brought up with: Father and Son, Mother and Child, the Holy Family, the City of God, the King and the Kingdom, and so on. When we pare all that away, when all that is dead, we shall be better placed to know Whom the social forms are veiling.

All my data are written words in published works, especially of the father and son. We should like to have the impossible: audio-visual records of the father's ongoing communication with his children or, better yet, of household scenes in the life of the family. We might like the same sort of records of Schreber himself, before and during his "nervous illness." And we should like to know more about his marriage, of which he says so little. I should have wished to sample with my own sensory organs the pageant of stimuli emitted by the persons and objects in his first and second families and his hospital ward. And how was Schreber's father brought up? And his mother? And *their* parents? Our available data are a tiny fragment of a fragment of the information we might like to obtain. Still, what we have is enough for my purposes here.

There are benefits in studying written words. Unlike people, they are uninfluenced by the fact of being observed. Anyone now or years hence can repeat precisely my relations to the situation I have investigated. And Schreber's autobiography has the advantage of being more complete than a case history ever is. It is thorough, rich in detail, and elaborated so subtly that Schreber himself said it would have been hard to render its ideas by word of mouth (*Memoirs*, p. 275).

We are fortunate to have Schreber's book. Had he experienced and behaved as he did in a hospital today, he would have qualified for a barrage of antischizophrenia treatment: high doses of tranquilizers, electroshocks or insulin comas or both, and possibly brain surgery. His treatment would have hindered or prevented his writing. In his thirteen years in hospitals he received, as far as we know, only narcotic and sedative drugs.

I venture in this study into the traditional preserve of psychiatry; for instance, I offer theories about hallucinations, hypochondriasis, and paranoia and I derive my data from the case of someone who is considered a classic mental patient. But this book is also about *politics:* the micro-politics of child-rearing and family life and their relation to the macro-politics of larger human groups. In calling into question the value of the mental illness model, in its classic form, as a means of understanding someone like Schreber, I also raise issues pertaining to the politics of psychiatry and medicine.

Political revolutions begin with a growing sense, often limited to a small part of the political community, that existing institutions have ceased to meet adequately problems posed by the environment they have in part created. Similarly, scientific revolutions start with a developing feeling, often restricted to a small number of scientists, that a prevailing paradigm no longer explains well enough some aspect of the world to which it may previously have led the way (Kuhn, 1970, pp. 92–93). As the decision to overthrow existing political structures entails the need to supply others, so the choice to attack a scientific model must involve a search for new ones.

In politics and law we are in the power of our rulers; in our habits of thinking and seeing we are in the power of our premises. Hence, we had better choose them well.

Many investigators regard someone seen as schizophrenic as a victim of events whose origin lies within himself. They do not look upon his "condition" as a response to conduct toward him of people around him; on the contrary, they may assume he has been "out of contact" with others, possibly from birth. The evidence I present in this book demands and embodies a shift away from that viewpoint. I offer no polished model for understanding people called schizophrenic; it is too soon for that. Rather, I move along and point to routes by which the old model might be changed or new ones found.

Many people are baffled by the behavior of persons seen as schizophrenic. I suggest that were they to meet in depth, individually and as a "family," as I have, the persons composing the families of such persons, they might find them no less bewildering than the so-called psychotic offspring. It would, I expect, become easy to see that to be able to live in such families might require special, devious, and even bizarre strategies.

In the next few chapters I shall describe close-up the thinking of the father of a schizophrenic son. Learning the father's views can be disconcerting. I find it painful to imagine living with him and terrifying to think of growing up in his household. Yet he enjoyed the high esteem of his colleagues and contemporaries for at least several decades and influenced many people. That is what gives this story importance going far beyond the usual concerns of clinical psychiatry.

13

THE
FATHER

Dr. Daniel Gottlieb Moritz Schreber, the father of the eminent
mental patient, was an unusual man. He wrote books about
human anatomy and physiology, hygiene and physical culture.
He was devoted to body-building by gymnastics: he exercised
daily and had parallel and horizontal bars built in his garden;
he founded a gymnastic association, had a gymnasium built for
it, and successfully urged student associations to force their
members to join it (Ritter, 1936, pp. 10, 18). He added moral
principles to his precepts for physical health, joining them in a
comprehensive educational system for parents and teachers. He
said he used his methods upon his own children. He believed
that if readers of his books applied his ideas to their daily lives
and their children's, a stronger race of men would result. He
dedicated one book of his, from which I quote much, "to the
salvation of future generations." The full title of the book is
*Education Toward Beauty by Natural and Balanced Further-
ance of Normal Body Growth, of Life-Supporting Health, and
of Mental Ennoblement, Especially by the Use, if Possible, of
Special Educational Means: for Parents, Educators, and Teachers.*
   In the 1840s the young doctor planned to build a sanatorium
for children but failed, despite much effort, to gain permission

15

from the authorities (Ritter, p. 18). At thirty-six he became the medical director of an orthopedic institute in Leipzig, a post he held until he died at fifty-three. At his death, his son Daniel Paul, the author of the *Memoirs*, was nineteen.

Freud, writing in 1911, the year the son died and fifty years after the father's death, said about the father:

> [He] was no insignificant person . . . [his] memory is kept green to this day by the numerous Schreber Associations which flourish especially in Saxony. . . . His activities in favour of promoting the harmonious upbringing of the young, of securing co-ordination between educators in the home and in the school, of introducing physical culture and manual work with a view to raising the standards of health—all this exerted a lasting influence upon his contemporaries. His great reputation as the founder of therapeutic gymnastics in Germany is still shown by the wide circulation of his *Ärztliche Zimmergymnastik* (Medical Indoor Gymnastics) in medical circles and the numerous editions through which it has passed. (*Standard Edition, 12,* p. 51)

The Schreber Associations Freud mentions are societies for calisthenics, gardening, and fresh-air activities; Niederland (1960) says that in 1958 there were over two million members in Germany. Dr. Schreber also began the Schreber Gardens: small plots of land near the outskirts of cities, which city-dwellers own and, on weekends, till; they are still widespread in Germany and parts of Switzerland.

Possibly, Dr. Schreber had one face for the world and another for those with whom he lived. Franz Baumeyer (1956), a German psychoanalyst, while in charge of a hospital near Dresden from 1946 to 1949, found this note among case records of the son's hospitalizations: "His father (founder of the Schreber Gardens in Leipzig) suffered from obsessional ideas with murderous impulses." Baumeyer thinks its source was a member of the Schreber family or a person close to the family (Niederland, 1960); the father had died thirty years before the note was written.

Dr. Schreber had two sons. Daniel Gustav, three years older than his brother, Daniel Paul, shot and killed himself at thirty-eight (Niederland, 1963). Daniel Gustav's youngest sister said he had had a "progressive psychosis" and that a doctor had thought of placing him in an asylum (Baumeyer, 1956); a newspaper obituary said he had been melancholic (Niederland, 1963). Daniel Gustav's nephew, the son of the eldest sister, Anna, told Baumeyer (1956) that Daniel Gustav had "started studying law and ended up with chemistry"; this seems to conflict with the newspaper obituary Niederland quotes, which says Daniel Gustav was a judge.

Little is known about Dr. Schreber's wife, their other children (three daughters), or their family life. One of the daughters is labeled hysterical in the hospital records Baumeyer found (*ibid.*). The same nephew told Baumeyer that Sidonie, the daughter immediately younger than Daniel Paul, remained unmarried and at the end was "mentally no longer quite right"; we do not know if Sidonie is the "hysterical" daughter.

Anna, in a letter she wrote in 1909, two years after her mother's death, describes her mother's role:

> Father discussed with our mother everything and anything; she took part in all his ideas, plans, and projects, she read the galley proofs of his writings with him, and was his faithful, close companion in everything. (*Niederland, 1963,* p. 203)

We can infer from Dr. Schreber's writings what sort of role his wife played:

> When the man can support his opinions by reason of demonstrable truth, no wife with common sense and good will will want to oppose his decisive voice (D. G. M. Schreber, 1858, p. 32n);

> If one wants a planned upbringing based on principles to flourish, the father above anyone else must hold the reins of upbringing in his hands. . . . The main responsibility for the whole

result of upbringing always belongs to the father. . . .(*Ibid.*, p. 32)

For Dr. Schreber there was one supreme being—God, who is male. He advised teaching children that God is "the loving Father of the world" (p. 155).

I quote Niederland's (1963) further report of Anna's letter:

> She describes in it in some detail how everything in the Schreber home was *Gottwärts gerichtet* (orientated towards God), how God was present in their childhood world at all times, not merely in their daily prayers, but in all their feeling, thinking, and doings. She concludes the letter with the words: "All this was finished with the sudden death of our beloved father. . . ." (p. 205)

In her view, and in her view of other family members' views, God's presence in the home depended upon their father's presence. Given Dr. Schreber's views about the parts fathers do and must play in families, it is likely he held God-like power in his family. Family members, who connected his presence with God's, were probably representing the family power system in cosmic terms. And the father, seen by them as God and enacting the role of God, taught them with his "divine" authority that God is Father.

Dr. Schreber urged parents to urge, encourage, and induce children to be devoted to God.

> It is just as well that these youngsters learn to appreciate at an early stage that every human being is duty-bound to accept that everything that transcends the realm of his own power rests upon the dispensation of a Higher Hand. (1858, p. 244)

If a child's father is his God, and he learns that everything which transcends his own power rests upon God's, then his father's power over him increases even more.

I propose (as Freud did) that the author of the *Memoirs* transfigured the father of his childhood into the God of his "nervous illness." Throughout this book I display links between the father's probable behavior toward his son and the son's strange relations with God.

Dr. Schreber thought parents must curtail their children's freedom by harsh disciplines. It was for the sake of health: moral, mental, and physical. He seemed to believe that children are criminal or ill from the start, or surely would become so unless rescued in time. For instance, he suggests (1860) "compelling" teachers "by school law" to invite parents to regular meetings at school and gives this among his reasons:

> This arrangement would enable the citizens to hear both sides instead of only the laments and lies of the pupils. The increasingly prevalent motives of pupils to wish to deceive the teacher or the parents or both would be nipped in the bud. The pupils, their consciousness being under uniform, close, mutual control would be morally uplifted. . . . (p. 41)

The pupils would not be invited.

His model of the human mind is simple. Thoughts, feelings, and acts are either good, noble, high, right, and fine, or bad, ignoble, low, wrong, and crude. Those that are neither are "indifferent." He presumes to know what is good, noble, high, right, and fine and what is not; he does not say how he knows. Bad elements of the mind are "weeds" to be "uprooted" and "exterminated."

> The noble seeds of human nature sprout upwards in their purity almost on their own if the ignoble ones, the weeds, are sought out and destroyed in time. This must be done ruthlessly and vigorously. It is a dangerous error to believe that flaws in a child's character will disappear by themselves. The blunt edges may disappear but the root remains, shows itself in poisoned impulses, and has a damaging effect on the noble tree of life. A child's misbehaviour will become in the adult a serious fault in character and opens the way to vice and baseness. (1858, p. 140)

He felt humanity to be beleaguered by adversaries, namely weakness, sensuality, indolence, softness, and cowardice. He thought it

19

especially important and crucial for the whole of life with regard to character . . . to form a protective wall against the unhealthy predominance of the emotional side, against that feeble sensitiveness—the disease of our age, which must be recognised as the usual reason for the increasing frequency of depression, mental illness, and suicide. (*Ibid.*, p. 281)

Ironically, depression and mental illness plagued his two sons and led to the suicide of one. In talking of "true nobility of soul" he could soar:

> Youthful imagination is best awakened or, if already aflame, given nourishment and direction through examples in which are mirrored moral purity, self-denial, humility before God and respect for men, kindheartedness, manly heroic spirit or noble womanhood, high-minded thoughts, complete fearlessness, maturity of mind, inflexible firmness of character in the whirlpool of temptations, brave determination, vigorous energy, unflagging but moderate persistence in the striving for high noble aims, steadfastness in danger and pain—in short, all aspects of true nobility of soul. (p. 291)

He thinks it critical to start training early. With babies of five to six months parents must follow the "law of habituation," "the most general law for mental education of this age group":

> *Suppress everything* in the child, keep everything away from him that he should not make his own, and guide him perseveringly towards everything to which he should habituate himself.

> If we habituate the child to the Good and Right we prepare him to do the Good and the Right later with consciousness and out of free will. . . . The habit is only a necessary precondition to make possible and facilitate the proper aim of *self-determination* of free will. . . . If one lets the wrongly directed habits take root the child is easily put in danger; even if he later recognises the Better he will not have the power anymore to suppress the wrongly directed habit. . . . (p. 60)

A stitch in time saves nine. If one does one's work early and well, one needs to do none, or nearly none, later. One will be able to leave the children to follow "freely" what they have been taught.

Compare what his son said years later:

> The fundamental view I gained about God's relation to His creation is this: God executed His power of miracles on our earth . . . only until the ultimate aim of His creation was attained with the creation of the human being. From then on He left the created organic world as it were to itself, and interfered directly by miracles only very rarely, if at all, in very exceptional cases. (*Memoirs*, p. 191)

Dr. Schreber defines for parents what "the Good and Right" is for a child. To "habituate" a child means to program him to obey Dr. Schreber's views. Parents in this system doubly determine the child's self: they impose upon him the rule of obedience and create situations in which he must practice it.

Self-determination means that self, not someone else, determines who self is. Dr. Schreber means by it (and by "self-reliance" and "free will") that state in which one no longer needs parents to determine oneself, since they have already done so. His psycho-logic is peculiar; parents, in order to make a child self-determined, must first subdue the child's "self-will." He has no faith that a child could learn when and how to regulate his own behavior without being forced to.

Not surprisingly, his son attained the *exact* opposite of what is usually meant by self-determination. Dr. Weber, who was superintendent of the asylum in which Schreber was confined years later, wrote in a report that Schreber had *no "unimpaired self-determination* or sensible reasoning, rather the patient was completely under the power of overwhelming pathological influences" (Postscript to *Memoirs*, p. 278).

Dr. Schreber talks here about infants under one year:

> Our entire effect on the direction of the child's will at this time will consist in accustoming it to absolute obedience, which

21

has been in great part prepared for already by the applications of the principles laid down previously. . . . The thought should never even occur to the child that his will could be in control, rather should the habit of subordinating his will to the will of his parents or teachers be immutably implanted in him. . . . There is then joined to the feeling of law a feeling of impossibility of struggling against the law; a child's obedience, the basic condition for all further education, is thus solidly founded for the time to come. (1858, p. 66)

Parents must have already made it a rule for the child at five or six months to obey them. Now, while he is still under a year, they must make it a rule that he never think of disobeying or think it possible to disobey. To "educate" a child means for Dr. Schreber, as we shall see, to impose a rule upon every detail of his life. The more control and obedience, the more "moral will power."

Moral will power is the sword of victory in the coming battle of life. Be not afraid, loving parents, at these words. The true and high goal of human life can and should be achieved only through noble battling . . . We cannot and should not spare them [children] this fight, for it is the basic condition of life; without this fight there can be no triumph and without this no true happiness in life. But we can and should equip them as best we can with the weapon with which to conduct the fight with dignity, in order to achieve the elevated success of victory—and this weapon with which they can enter life with joyful spirits is precisely moral will power. (*Ibid.*, p. 134)

Dr. Schreber is in battle against parts of himself and of children. The enemy is within. Parents, he says, must ally themselves with children against children's selves and equip them with a "weapon" for "battle." "Victory" for him means to suppress possibilities of experience and behavior *he* regards as dangers. But in a fight pitting a self against itself, self cannot win without also losing.

He continues:

> Now, the ways and means of developing and consolidating moral will power and character do not need to be sought. . . . The most generally necessary condition for the attainment of this goal is the *unconditional obedience* of the child. (p. 135; italics in original)

The child arrives at this goal with his parents' prior and present help.

> If the child had been led in the first stage of development [before one year old] along the path towards habituation to unconscious obedience, so now [after one] is it timely and indispensable for the attainment of the noble aim of upbringing, that this habit should be gradually raised to an act of free will, that obedience is conscious. The child should be trained . . . to noble independence and full strength of his own will. The transition is much facilitated by previous habituation. (p. 135)

The child is "trained" to "noble independence," a state which previous habits of obedience make easier to reach. Dr. Schreber uses a trick (probably unwittingly): he calls the unfreedom the child reaches "noble independence." Dr. Schreber's thoughts on the matter involve more twists:

> The child must gradually learn to recognise more and more that he has the *physical possibility* of wishing and acting otherwise, but that he *elevates himself through his own independence* to the *moral impossibility* of wishing or acting otherwise. This is achieved partly by a short statement of the reasons for precepts and prohibitions, as far as this is appropriate and feasible (for the child must also, of course, acquiesce and obey unconditionally, sometimes when a statement of reasons has to be withheld); partly also by illustrative references to the freedom of will present in the child: "You could act differently, but a good child does not want to act differently." . . . (p. 135)

The child, "physically" free now, unlike before, to wish to disobey and to disobey parents, must learn the "moral impossibility" of either; he becomes free in potential, not in practice.

The child must think he "elevates himself through his own independence" to reach this state, while in fact the parent brings him to it. The parent's statement in this passage can be decomposed into its secret, elementary premises: "You could act differently, but I tell you who you are, and I say you are a child who (a) wishes to be good, (b) agrees with my definition of good, (c) does not see my definition to be mine only, and (d) suspects no secret premises in what I say." The aim is for the child to do what his *parent* wants, while thinking he does what *he* wants. Freedom is free not to be free and to see its unfreedom as freedom; that is all. It is not free to see how, why, or that it is being deceived. For Dr. Schreber no deception occurs since independence *is* obedience. When independence is *dis*obedience it must be crushed.*

> In the case of nearly every child, however, even the most well brought up, there are sometimes surprising manifestations of defiance or rebelliousness although if the discipline has been good these should occur only rarely—a vestige of that *innate barbarity* which leads the developing *self-confidence* astray. This mostly happens towards the end of the second year. The child suddenly and often quite surprisingly refuses what until now he has most willingly given—his obedience. This could be caused by anything—the most important thing is that the disobedience should be *crushed* to the point of regaining complete submission, using corporal punishment if necessary. (pp. 136–137)

---

* Dr. Schreber in these passages is asserting views compatible with much nineteenth-century thinking. Many people believed then, and some still do, that when "passion" moves us to act our acts are not free since passion is *causing* them. In this view we must and can resist "passion" with our "wills": only "reason" or "conscience" guides us to true freedom, and we attain "true" freedom as distinct from caprice, or "false" freedom, by obeying moral laws. The Hegelians went further and identified moral law with the law of the state so that "true" freedom meant obeying the police. Bertrand Russell (1961) points out that this philosophy or psychology was based upon the false premise that a passion is a cause, whereas a desire, for whatever reason, to be virtuous is not (p. 126).

24

He assumes that "self-confidence" depends upon not defying or rebelling against discipline; trust of self depends upon not expressing distrust of parents. He betrays here his previous play with the word "freedom." He is ruled by a wish to oppress, or a fear of not oppressing, children.

A child raised by his system, as I illustrate throughout this book, is subject to parental authority, especially a father's, all day every day until at least twenty; Dr. Schreber's guidebook (1858) for comprehensive control of children explicitly applies to children from birth to twenty.

Schreber's entire madness is an *image* of his father's war against his independence. He is never free of coercion by what he thinks are external spiritual powers. However, he never connects the coercion with his father. A reason why might be that his father masked (probably unawares) the source of control, by defining the state of being controlled by parents as *self-control*.

Parents and teachers, like writers of computer programs, build certain sorts of information more deeply and irreversibly than others into their systems (children): in the idiom of computer engineers they hard-program them. What is hard-programmed cannot easily be changed; to do so would mean a drastic reorganizing of the system. Programmers (such as parents or teachers) tend to hard-program items they do not anticipate should ever need to be altered. They soft-program components of the program (or education) they think may have to be modified at some future time. They are guided in their choice of what they hard-program or soft-program by what they expect will be the future applications of the program. Generally they try to hard-program instructions about abstract, general forms (e.g., "respect your parents," "love God"), while soft-programming items of a more specific type referring to details of content ("don't eat with your fingers," "shine your shoes"). They hard-program many premises about relationships.

It has been a major discovery of psychoanalysis that patterns of relations with other people that are programmed earliest in life are often programmed hardest. People tend to repeat "compulsively" all their lives forms of relating that were prefigured in infancy. The phenomenon of "transference," by which someone's experience of and behavior toward a therapist is modeled upon one's earliest relations with significant other people, is a striking example. Wilhelm Reich seems to refer by "armouring" to the display by and in one's body of hard-programs about sexual relationships.

When Dr. Schreber urges the suppression of infants under one, he is consciously and deliberately hard-programming them to obey their parents robotlike for as long as they know them. His aim: "unconditional obedience" to parents as an abstract general principle to apply in all contexts in all families.

He sees a child trained to obey parents unconditionally as "nobly independent" and likely would have induced a child to see himself similarly. While teaching a child to do what his parents wish, Dr. Schreber teaches him to think that he does what he, the child, wishes and makes it hard for the child to see he is still doing what his parents wish, which might be what the child would *not* wish, were he able to think clearly. Dr. Schreber seems unaware that he is misrepresenting submission as freedom; he appears to see submission *as* freedom.

Dr. Schreber's system implies a contradiction, which he does not seem to see, between where it trains a child to look for his programs and where it trains him to *think* he looks. It teaches the child to expect an external authority to program him ("the habit of subordinating his will to the will of his parents or teachers" must be "immutably implanted in him"), but also teaches him to see himself as "self-reliant" and "self-determined," i.e., as the origin of his programming.

Since Schreber, the son, would have been confronted with this contradiction as a small boy, he could not have coped with it by leaving the situation.

Certain experiences of the son in his "nervous illness" can be

26

seen as an ingenious attempt to deal with the contradiction. This view of his experiences is radically different from the view that they are signs and symptoms of an illness, as the concept of illness has been classically understood.*

Through "rays," the son's God watches, dictates, or condemns his every move, all day every day, much as, it seems, his father had done. The son feels God and the "rays" to be at once outside *and* inside himself. He sees them with his

> *bodily* eye when I keep my eyes open

and with his

> *mind's* eye when my eyes are closed by miracles or when I close them voluntarily. (*Memoirs*, p. 227)

In this way he experiences himself subject to outside authority, as in fact he was taught to be, *and* as "self-determined," as he was taught to regard himself. The external programmer of his childhood is again located outside the son's self as God, *and* the son is also "self-determined" in a special sense:

> I receive light and sound sensations which are projected direct on to my *inner* nervous system by the rays. (*Ibid.*, p. 117)

---

* The concept of illness is evolving. Even classic diseases such as tuberculosis and heart attacks are now seen as the end result of a long, complex series of events some of which belong to the domains of psychology and sociology.

Is someone who deals with *others'* disturbing behavior in ways that lead him to be labeled mentally ill "really" ill? This issue has far-reaching practical implications for the lives of psychiatrists, mental patients, and possibly all of us. I think much of the *theoretical* argument turns on how broadly or narrowly the word "illness" is defined.

III

THE FATHER'S
METHODS

Some of you may have begun to see Dr. Schreber as laying
the basis for a system of child *persecution*, not child education.
He and many of his contemporaries saw his system as working
toward saving mankind. They would have dismissed your view
as invalid. Dr. Schreber might have seen it as evidence of your
"feeble sensitiveness," occasioned by your parents' failure to
uproot the "weeds" of your nature as a child.

Here he gives details of his methods:

> . . . One must look at the moods of the little ones that are
> announced by screaming without reason and crying. . . . If one
> has convinced oneself that no real need, no disturbing or painful
> condition, no sickness is present, one can be assured that the
> screaming is only and simply the expression of a mood, a whim,
> the first appearance of self-will. . . . One has to step forward in
> a positive manner: by quick distraction of the attention, stern
> words, threatening gestures, rapping against the bed . . . or,
> when all this is of no avail: by moderate, intermittent, bodily
> admonishments consistently repeated until the child calms down
> or falls asleep. . . .

> Such a procedure is necessary only once or at most twice and—
> one is *master* of the child *forever*. From now on a glance, a

word, a single threatening gesture, is sufficient to rule the child. One should keep in mind that one shows the child the greatest kindness in this, in that one saves him from many hours of tension, which hinder him from thriving, and also frees him from all those inner spirits of torment that very easily grow up vigorously into more serious and insurmountable enemies of life. (1858, pp. 60–61)

Dr. Schreber presupposes that a parent's goal is to master the child. The child must be mastered in order to be saved from *Dr. Schreber's* view of a child's self. *Dr. Schreber* sees "tensions" and "inner spirits of torment" in a child who cries, which *he* thinks are precursors of "insurmountable enemies of life." This is how he justifies "saving" the child. *He* sees the child's crying as "crying without reason" because he sees no reason for it. The child could be crying because he is bored and wants someone to play with him. *He* thinks a "whim" in a five- or six-month-old is a bad sign. He does not see that an infant's wish to win a response to his whims could be a real need.

A psychoanalytic interpretation would be that Dr. Schreber projects "inner spirits of torment" from inside himself into a child, i.e., he thinks he wants to master a child but really wants to master "bad" parts of himself. Many psychoanalysts have dwelled upon the motives of the person who projects; few have pondered the experience of the person *upon whom* someone else projects parts of himself, which he tries to master "in" the other person for what he imagines is the other's sake. Here is the son's experience:

> God Himself was on *my* side in *His* fight *against me*, that is to say I was able to bring *His* attributes and powers into battle as an effective weapon in *my* self-defence. (*Memoirs*, p. 79n)

Dr. Schreber talks everywhere of parents changing children, not of parents learning from children. The channel of effects is one-way. The child in Dr. Schreber's system would find it almost impossible to bring about a change in the system being applied to him. Dr. Schreber's son, to alter the situation, would have had to see that his father was beset by "tension," "inner spirits of torment," and "insurmountable enemies," why he was so beset, and how to help his father to see it—not an easy job for a child.

The son writes:

> It is an extremely difficult question even for me to explain this inability on the part of God to learn by experience. (*Ibid.*, p. 154)

and:

> *A long time ago* I formulated the idea that God cannot learn by experience in written notes as follows: "Every attempt at an educative influence must be given up as hopeless." Every day which has since passed has confirmed the correctness of this opinion. (p. 155)

Dr. Schreber's mind is tied up with saving children from what he sees as dangers—physical, mental, and moral. He seems to care for little else. Similarly, God in the son's "nervous illness" appears to have no life apart from His relation to him. God, the son says,

> had tied Himself to a single human being. . . . (p. 252)

Dr. Schreber cannot be free of battle on behalf of children. Indeed, since what he is fighting is within himself, how could he be free?

Dr. Schreber says:

> If the child is lifted from the bed and carried around each time he makes noises—without checking if there is really something wrong—and is calmed by gentleness of one kind or another, this may often lead to the appearance of the emotion of spite later in the life of the child. I wish mothers and nursemaids would recognise the importance of this point! (1858, p. 61)

He deploys the term "spite" against a child who refuses a position his parent assigns him. In his view, the child who shows

31

spite is bad; the child a parent can rule by "a glance," "a word," "a single threatening gesture" is good. Since he gives no evidence that lifting an infant and carrying him around whenever he makes noises may "often lead" to "spite" later—nor does any exist as far as I know—I assume that what he fears is his fancy.

> . . . Another important rule: even allowed desires of the child should be fulfilled only if they are expressed in a friendly, harmless, or at least quiet manner, never if by screaming or unruly movements . . . even if the child's need for his regular feeding is the cause. . . . One has to keep from the child even the faintest glimmer that he could, by screaming or unruly behaviour, force anything from his environment . . . The child learns very soon that only by . . . self control he gains his purpose. (*Ibid.*, p. 62)

Is a five- or six-month-old free to choose to express his wants "quietly," as Dr. Schreber seems to think? An infant at this age is physiologically unable to specify some needs, especially hunger, sometimes, without screaming or waving his arms and legs; a demand for "self-control" would frustrate and confuse him. If his appeals were not endorsed, he might stop trying. Dr. Schreber says that "service personnel seldom have enough comprehension" to share these ideas of his and practice them. Maybe they comprehended more than he did.

> By the last mentioned habit the child has already a noticeable headstart in the art of waiting and is ready for . . . an even more important one, the art of self-denial. . . . Each forbidden desire—whether or not it is to the child's disadvantage—must be consistently and unfailingly opposed by an unconditional refusal. The refusal of a desire alone is not enough though; one has to see to it that the child receives this refusal calmly and if necessary, one has to make this calm acceptance a firm habit by using a stern word or threat, etc. Never make an exception from this! . . . This is the only way to make it easy for the child to attain the salutary and indispensable habit of subordination and control of his will. . . . (p. 63)

Why is it "salutary" and "indispensable" that a child, before he is one year old, learn how to subordinate his will and receive calmly the denial of his desires? Dr. Schreber does not say. Perhaps this is how *his* father taught him "self-denial" when *he* was an infant. Or was it his mother, or nurse?

Here is an example Dr. Schreber gives from his family. He is discussing "disciplinary behaviour towards children in cases of illness." Since he is talking of a male infant, he could be referring to the author of the *Memoirs:*

> One of my children had fallen ill at the age of one and a half, and the only treatment, though a dangerous one, giving any hope for saving his life was possible only through the completely quiet submissiveness of the young patient. It succeeded, because the child had been accustomed from the beginning to the most absolute obedience towards me, whereas otherwise the child's life would in all probability have been beyond any chance of rescue. (p. 67)

It would be interesting to know how the child's absolute obedience toward his father made possible the only treatment that could save his life, and what that treatment was. It is unlikely we can ever find out.

A parent's demand does not always need a rationale, Dr. Schreber thinks, as in the next example. Might makes right.

> If one asks a child to hand something to oneself with one specific hand but the child will use only the other hand, the intelligent upbringer will not rest until the act is done as demanded and the impure motive is removed. (p. 137)

The irrelevance of the parent's demand is irrelevant to Dr. Schreber. He never considers it possible that a child who opts to disobey a parent's arbitrary wish may know, better than his parent, what is best for him.

In Dr. Schreber's view, a parent must do more than control a child's acts. He must control his *"sentiments,"* his *"motives."* The "outer" is less important than the "inner."

Let us always treat the child exactly as his sentiments, which are mirrored so clearly in the whole of his being, deserve. . . . If parents stay true to themselves with this principle, they will soon be rewarded by the appearance of a wonderful relationship where the child is nearly always ruled merely by parental glances. (pp. 137–138)

Dr. Schreber seems to be saying that as parents raise their power over their children they will be "rewarded" by the possibility of greater power still; the goal is for the child to be in a sort of trance in which he experiences a glance of the parent as a command. Why is that relationship wonderful? And for whom?

Although Dr. Schreber thinks the child must be rewarded or punished not only for his acts, but for the sentiments underlying them, he thinks the child must not obey in order to get praise or reward. He thinks a wish for praise or reward is a "degraded" and "impure" sentiment. He compares certain rewards to "poison" (p. 139). Nor must the child obey because he fears punishment. *And* he must not obey while secretly *wishing* to disobey; that would be dishonesty—a bad sentiment. He must obey because he knows it is right to obey, no matter how whimsical is his parent's wish.

To tailor his consciousness to meet the demands of this system, a child would have to deny, repress, split, project, displace, etc., much of his experience. Even having done so, it is hard to see how he could think, in some situations, any thought without breaking a rule.

The son in his *Memoirs* says that God, whom he experiences as irresistibly attracted to him, is able to withdraw from him only when he, the son, stops thinking. He may be remembering his relationship with his father without realizing it; to realize it would be to think a forbidden thought. The father sought to crush so many thoughts in children that his son might have thought, had he been allowed to think it, that his father would leave him alone only if he stopped thinking.

The son experiences his thinking and all else about himself

34

as under alien surveillance, for instance by means of the "writing-down-system":

> Books or other notes are kept in which for years have been
> written down all my thoughts, all my phrases, all my necessaries,
> all the articles in my possession or around me, all persons with
> whom I come into contact, etc. . . . I presume that the writing
> down is done by creatures given human shape on distant celestial
> bodies . . . , but lacking all intelligence; their hands are led
> automatically, as it were, by passing rays for the purpose of
> making them write down, so that later rays can again look at
> what has been written. (*Memoirs*, p. 119)

> The writing-down-system . . . became a mental torture, from
> which I suffered severely for years and to which I am only
> slowly getting a little accustomed; because of it, I had to endure
> trials of patience as they have probably never before had to be
> borne by a human being, . . . (*Ibid.*, pp. 122–123)

Later he decides that "God Himself" must "have started the
system of writing down."

Clinically, the "writing-down-system" is a paranoid delusion.
Note how it becomes intelligible in the light of this passage by
Schreber's father:

> In families . . . a quite effective means of education is a punish-
> ment board, which is to be stuck upon the wall of the children's
> room. Such a board would list the children's names and against
> them every committed misdeed: all ever so little signs of omis-
> sion, all instances of insubordination, would be chalked up by a
> tick or by a remark. At the end of each month everybody would
> assemble for the hour of reckoning. According to what tran-
> spired, reproach or praise would be assigned. If one or other of
> the children had shown some recurring faults or weaknesses,
> particular mentions would be made of these. It is indeed sur-
> prising what moral effect such a board has on the children, even
> the less naughty and more indifferent ones. This is so, because
> the board is constantly in front of them, because every misdeed

that has been committed remains as a sort of *permanent* visual warning in front of their eyes for a considerable period of time. By this method many otherwise necessary educational steps, reminders, corrections, and punishments need not be applied and can be replaced in a far more efficient manner. (1858, pp. 264–265)

In reexperiencing these events, the son changes their venue from his family of origin to a celestial context; his father's punishment board has become God's "writing-down-system." Why did he do it? Had he not replaced "my father himself" with "God Himself" as the source of the "system," he could have avoided giving others the chance to see him as mad, at least in this regard. It is unlikely that he had forgotten, by the ordinary amnesia for events of early childhood, his father's role in the "writing-down-system"; his father recommends the punishment board for children seven to sixteen years old.

Possibly, his "forgetting" might be connected with his knowledge, conscious or not, that his father would have seen as impure and self-willed the bitterness and anger accompanying this memory that he, the son, might have felt toward his father. Were the son still a child, his father might have written down such feelings as a "permanent visual warning" until the "hour of reckoning." The son, probably still "habituated" and governed by his father's former responses to his "self-will," may have found it more forbidden to resent him than God.

Dr. Schreber's aim is to become "master of the child forever," to "rule the child" with only "a glance, a word, a single threatening gesture." It is a "wonderful relationship where the child is nearly always ruled merely by parental eye movements." His view of a good parent-child relationship is like the relation between a hypnotist and a subject in his power: a child who experiences a glance, a word, a gesture of the parent as a command resembles a person in a trance.

R. D. Laing and Aaron Esterson (1964), two Scottish psychiatrists, compare the prepsychotic state to hypnosis:

36

> Is the pre-psychotic child in some sense hypnotized by the parents, or is hypnosis an experimentally induced model psychosis, or, perhaps more precisely, an experimentally induced model pre-psychotic relationship? Experimental hypnosis certainly simulates some aspects of the pre-psychotic child-parent relationship. . . . (p. 73*n*)

Schreber, the son, compares his state, which he calls *"soul murder,"* to that of a hypnotic subject. In an open letter to his former doctor, P. E. Flechsig, which he prints as a preface to his *Memoirs,* he writes that "souls (rays)" deem it

> impermissible that a person's system should be influenced by another's to the extent of imprisoning his will power, such as occurs during hypnosis; in order to stress forcefully that this was a malpractice it was called "soul murder, . . ." (p. 35)

The term "soul murder," he says, is already in current usage and refers to the idea

> widespread in the folk-lore and poetry of all peoples that it is somehow possible to take possession of another person's soul. . . .
> (p. 55)

What is called psychosis may be, at least sometimes, an attempt gone awry to awaken from a daze in which one was put as a child. Schreber's father, it seems, had put his son to sleep, in a sense, in early childhood. The son partially awoke to this awareness while thought mad:

> At the time when my nervous illness seemed almost incurable, I gained the conviction that soul murder had been attempted on me by somebody. . . . (p. 55)

He cannot or will not, however, connect "soul murder" with his father. First he suspects Dr. Flechsig, his first hospital doctor, or Flechsig's "nerves" or "soul" as the "instigator" of "soul murder." Then he changes his view:

> It occurred to me only much later, in fact only while writing this essay did it become quite clear to me that God Himself

must have known of the plan, if indeed he was not the instigator, to commit soul murder on me. . . . (p. 77)

In searching for the murderer of his soul, Schreber came to see that behind the figure of Flechsig stood God. Could he have unpeeled another veil, he would have seen his father, I think, as the prime "instigator." Had he done so, he would have been less susceptible to being seen as insane. But his father, I believe, had made himself his "master" "forever" and would never have allowed such an "impure" thought. A feature of "soul murder," it seems, was forbidding the victim to identify his murderer correctly.

IV

MEMORIES AND HALLUCINATIONS

Quel est donc le phénomène de la croyance délirante?
—Il est, disons-nous, méconnaissance, avec ce que ce
terme contient d'antinomie essentielle. Car méconnaître
suppose une reconnaissance, comme le manifeste la mé-
connaissance systématique, où il faut bien admettre que
ce qui est nié soit en quelque façon reconnu.
. . . Il me paraît clair en effet que dans les sentiments
d'influence et d'automatisme, le sujet ne reconnaît pas
ses propres productions comme étant siennes. C'est en
quoi nous sommes tous d'accord qu'un fou est un fou.
Mais le remarquable n'est-il pas plutôt qu'il ait à en
connaître? et la question, de savoir ce qu'il connaît là
de lui sans s'y reconnaître?*

Jacques Lacan

O nobly-born, whatever fearful and terrifying visions
thou mayst see, recognize them to be thine own thought-
forms.

The Tibetan Book of the Dead

Schreber endured for many years during his "nervous illness"
painful and humiliating bodily experiences. He thought they
were "miracles [*Wunder*]," which God performed, through

---

* (What in fact is the phenomenon of delusional belief? It is, I insist, failure
to recognise, with all that this term contains of an essential paradox. For to
fail to recognise presupposes a recognition, as is manifested in systematic

"rays," upon his body. These experiences, and especially his view of their origin, led others to consider him crazy. Here he discusses them:

> From the first beginnings of my contact with God up to the present day my body has continuously been the object of divine miracles. If I wanted to describe all these miracles in detail I could fill a whole book with them alone. I may say that hardly a single limb or organ in my body escaped being temporarily damaged by miracles, nor a single muscle being pulled by miracles, either moving or paralysing it according to the respective purpose. Even now the miracles which I experience hourly are still of a nature to frighten every other human being to death; only by getting used to them through the years have I been able to disregard most of what happens as trivialities. But in the first year of my stay at Sonnenstein [the mental asylum] the miracles were of such a threatening nature that I thought I had to fear almost incessantly for my life, my health or my reason. (*Memoirs*, p. 131)

> This, as indeed the whole report about the miracles enacted upon my body, will naturally sound extremely strange to all other human beings, and one may be inclined to see in it only the product of a pathologically vivid imagination. In reply I can only give the assurance that hardly any memory from my life is more certain than the miracles recounted in this chapter. What can be more definite for a human being than what he has lived through and felt on his own body? (*Ibid.*, p. 132*n*.)

---

failure to recognise, where it must obviously be admitted that what is denied is in some fashion recognised.

. . . It seems clear to me that in his feelings of influence and automatism, the subject does not recognise his productions as his own. It is in this respect that we all agree that a madman is a madman. But isn't the remarkable part rather that he should have to take cognisance of them? And isn't the question rather to discover what he knows about himself in these productions without recognising himself in them?) "*Propos sur la causalité psychique*" (1950), pp. 33–34, quoted and translated by Wilden (1968), pp. 96–97.

These experiences caused him great suffering and interfered with everything he did. Here are five "miracles" he describes; I follow each of them with passages from his father's books:

Son:

"*Miracles of heat and cold* were and still are daily enacted against me . . . always with the purpose of preventing the natural feelings of bodily well-being. . . . During the *cold-miracle* the blood is forced out of the extremities, so causing a subjective feeling of cold . . . during the *heat-miracle* the blood is forced towards my face and head, in which of course coolness is the condition corresponding to a general sense of well-being. *From youth accustomed to enduring both heat and cold*, these miracles troubled me little . . . I myself have often been forced to seek heat and cold." (pp. 145–146)

Father:

". . . starting about three months after birth *cleansing of the infant's skin should be by cold ablutions only*, . . . in order to physically toughen up the child." (1852, p. 41)

He advises *warm baths for infants* up to six months. Then "one may pass to *cool and cold general ablutions*, which should be performed at least once daily and for which the body should be prepared by prior *local applications of cold water*" (*ibid.*, p. 40).

From the third year on "the purpose of health, which should now already be aiming more decisively at a corresponding toughening-up, is best achieved by *cold rubbings of the body*" (1858, p. 80). He says *cold baths* are the accepted rule after four or five years old.

"The bedroom should *no longer be heated at all* from the sixth to seventh year onwards." (*Ibid.*, p. 78)

He titled one of his books *The Cold-Water Healing Method* (1842).

41

Alfons Ritter (1936), who wrote a doctoral dissertation about Dr. Schreber, says that in Dr. Schreber's family of procreation "One strict rule was: one got up very early, did some gymnastics, bathed, and swam before starting work. Occasionally in winter the *ice had to be broken first*" (p. 12).

Son:

"My *eyes* and the *muscles of the lids* which serve to open and close them were an almost uninterrupted target for miracles. The eyes were always of particular importance. . . . The miracles on my eyes were performed by 'little men.' . . . These 'little men' were one of the most remarkable and even to me most mysterious phenomena. . . . Those occupied with the opening and closing of the eyes stood above the eyes in the eyebrows and there pulled the eyelids up or down as they pleased with fine filaments like cobwebs. . . . Whenever I showed signs of being unwilling to allow my eyelids to be pulled up and down and actually opposed it, the 'little men' became annoyed and expressed this by calling me 'wretch'; if I wiped them off my eyes with a sponge, it was considered by the rays as a sort of crime against God's gift of miracles.

"By the way wiping them away had only a very temporary effect, because the 'little men' were each time set down afresh . . . In order to prevent my closing or opening my eyes at will the thin layer of muscle situated in and above the eyelids and serving their movement has several times been removed by miracle." (*Memoirs*, pp. 136–138)

"As often as an insect . . . appears, a miracle simultaneously affects the *direction of my gaze*. I have not mentioned this miracle before, but it has been regularly practised for years. Rays after all continually *want to see what pleases them*. . . . My eye-muscles are therefore *influenced to move in a certain direction*. . . ." (*Ibid.*, pp. 186–187)

42

Father:
He insists on eye exercises for children in his booklet *The Systematically Planned Sharpening of the Sense Organs* (1859): to distract quickly a child's visual attention, to force him to estimate dimensions of similar objects at different distances, to judge various distances, etc. (p. 11). In another book (1858), in a section called "The Care, Education and Sharpening of Sense Organs," he recommends "the proper alternation between looking near and far. . . . One should get the children into the habit of recognizing the first traces of tiredness of the eyes, or of that well-known slightly burning or irritating feeling of overstimulation: in this case especially, besides rest, spraying the eyes with cool water is recommended; *repeated visual exercises* looking over mildly lit green areas with sharp or precise fixing on distant, barely recognizable objects, . . . Just as important are exercises in close-up vision, like precise observation and comparison of small objects. . . ." (p. 215)

He recommends that children's "eyelids, eyebrows, and temporal areas be treated daily with cold water," which he thinks will sharpen their vision (Niederland, 1959a, p. 387, quoted from D. G. M. Schreber, 1839).

Son:
He describes a painful experience he calls "the so-called coccyx miracle." "This was an extremely painful, caries-like state of the lowest vertebrae. Its purpose was *to make sitting and even lying down impossible.* Altogether I was not allowed to remain for long in *one and the same position* or at the same occupation: when I was walking one attempted to force me to lie down, and when I was *lying down one wanted to chase me off* my bed. Rays did not seem to appreciate at all that a human being who actually exists must be somewhere. . . . I had become an embarrassing being for the rays (for God), in whatever position or circumstance

43

I might be or whatever occupation I undertook." (*Memoirs*, p. 139)

Father:
He warns parents and educators to fight the child's tendency to sit unevenly because, he says, it harms the spinal column. ". . . One must see to it that children always sit straight and even-sided on both buttocks at once . . . leaning neither to the right nor left side. . . . As soon as they start to lean back . . . or bend their backs, the time has come to exchange at least for a few minutes the seated position for the absolutely still, supine one. If this is not done . . . the backbones will be deformed. . . ." (1858, p. 100)

". . . *Half resting in lying or wallowing positions should not be allowed:* if children are awake they should be alert and hold themselves in straight, active positions and be busy; in general each thing that could lead towards laziness and softness (for example the sofa in the children's room) should be kept away from their circle of activity." (*Ibid.*, p. 150)

These procedures and the following ones were part of the father's program to keep the bodies of children of all ages straight at all times: when they stood, sat, walked, played, lay down, or slept (see figures 1 and 2). He thought that children must sleep in a straight position only, flat on their backs; babies under four months must lie only on their backs when resting. It is important, he taught, to start with infants, since he thought it harder to train older children. In his book *The Harmful Body Positions and Habits of Children, Including a Statement of Counteracting Measures* (1853), he presented as medical fact his false idea that if a child lies too long on one side his body on that side may be damaged, "the nutrition is impaired," the "flow of juices is impeded," the "blood stops and piles up in the vessels," and the vessels "lose a large part of their life tension" (1858, p.

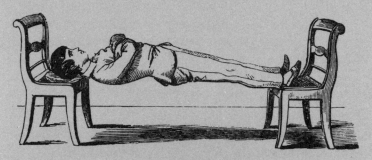

Figure 1 (p. 197) The "bridge." Dr. Schreber thought a forward slump of a child's head and shoulders when walking was "a clear expression of weakness, dumbness and cowardice." He devised the "bridge," an exercise "to strengthen the back and neck muscles" of children who slumped.

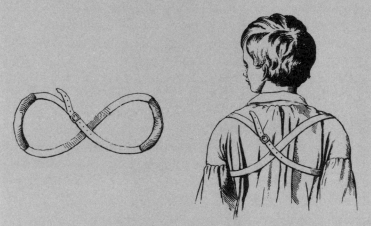

Figure 2 (p. 198) A shoulder band to prevent "falling forward of the shoulders." Dr. Schreber thought it should be worn every day, all day, until "the bad habit is regulated." The shaded parts of the band on the left are metal springs to rest on the front of the shoulders.

12). This may lead later to paralysis of the arm and foot on that side, he said (*ibid.*, p. 54).

Son:

"One of the most horrifying miracles was the so-called *compression-of-the-chest-miracle. . . ;* it consisted in the *whole chest wall being compressed,* so that the state of oppression caused by the lack of breath was transmitted to my whole body." (*Memoirs,* p. 133)

Father:

He invented a device called *Schrebersche Geradhalter* (Schreber's straight-holder) to force children to sit straight (see figures 3 and 4). This was an iron crossbar fastened to the table at which the child sat to read or write. The bar pressed against the collar bones and the front of the shoulders to prevent forward movements or crooked posture. He says the child could not lean for long against the bar "because of the *pressure* of the hard object against the bones and the consequent *discomfort;* the child will return on his own to the straight position" (1858, p. 204). "I had a *Geradhalter* manufactured which proved its worth *time and again with my own children . . .*" (*ibid.*, p. 203). He says that the vertical bar which supported it was useful too since it prevented young children from crossing their legs. "Checks in blood flow and other delicate reasons" make sitting with legs crossed "particularly wrong for youthful persons" (p. 201). (I discuss his views on children's genital pleasure in chapter VI.)

He also fastened a belt with ring-shaped shoulder straps to the child's bed. It ran across *the child's chest* to ensure that the child's body remained supine and straight when sleeping (see figures 5 and 6). The aim was to prevent "turning and tossing to either side."

Son:

"This was perhaps the most abominable of all miracles—

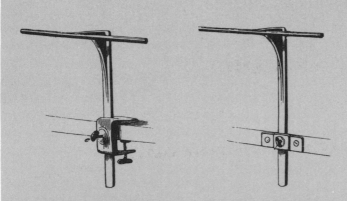

Figure 3 (p. 203) The Geradhalter. *On the left is a portable one for home use. The one on the right was fixed to desks at school.*

Figure 4 (p. 205) The Geradhalter *in use.*

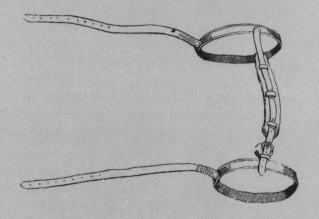

Figure 5 (p. 174) A belt for the sleeping child.

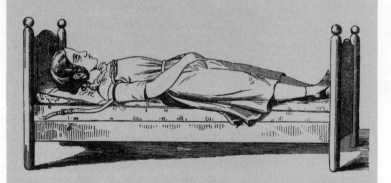

Figure 6 (174) The belt in use.

next to the compression-of-the-chest-miracle; the expression used for it if I remember correctly was 'the head-compressing-machine.' [*Kopfzusammenschnürungsmaschine:* literally, the head-together-tying machine]. . . . The 'little devils' . . . *compressed my head as though in a vice* by turning a kind of screw, causing my head temporarily to assume an elongated almost pear-shaped form. It had an extremely threatening effect, particularly as it was accompanied by severe pain. The screws were loosened temporarily but only very gradually, so that the *compressed state usually continued for some time.*" (*Memoirs*, p. 138)

"I suffer from almost uninterrupted headaches of a kind certainly unknown to other human beings, and hardly comparable to ordinary headaches. They are *tearing* and *pulling* pains." (*Ibid.*, p. 201)

Father:
He invented a *Kopfhalter* (head-holder) to prevent the child's head from falling forward or sideways. The *Kopfhalter* was a strap clamped at one end to the child's hair and at the other to his underwear so that it *pulled* his hair if he did not hold his head straight (see figure 7). It served as a "reminder" to keep the head straight: "The consciousness that the head cannot lean forward past a certain point soon becomes a habit." "This instrument can similarly be used against a sideways posture of the head." He admits it was apt to produce "*a certain stiffening effect on the head*" and should therefore be used only one or two hours a day (1858, pp. 198–199).

He also had a chin band made, which was held to the head by a helmetlike device (see figure 8). This was to ensure proper growth of the jaw and teeth (*ibid.*, pp. 219–220).

Son:
"Every word spoken near or with me, every human action

49

Figure 7 (p. 199)
The Kopfhalter.

Figure 8 (p. 220)
The chin band.

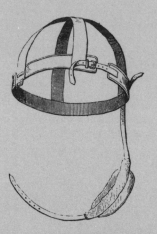

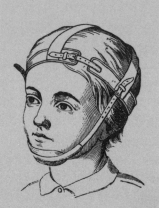

however small which is combined with some noise, for instance opening the door-locks on my corridor, pressing the latch on the door of my room, . . . etc., is accompanied by a painful blow directed at my head; the sensation of pain is like a sudden *pulling* inside my head which calls forth a very unpleasant feeling . . . and may be combined with the tearing off of part of the bony substance of my skull—at least that is how it feels." (*Memoirs*, p. 164)

Possibly upon hearing a sound he turned his head toward its source and reexperienced or remembered the pulling of the *Kopfhalter* when he had turned his head as a child.

These comparisons show uncanny similarities. It is as if the father taught his son a language of sensory stimuli by which to experience parts of his own body.*

Niederland wonders if Schreber's experiences of having been tied and strapped by the father into orthopedic apparatus are the origin of the "divine miracles" of "being tied-to-earth" and "fastened-to-rays."

> God is inseparably tied to my person through my nerves' power of attraction which for some time past has been inescapable; there is no possibility of God freeing Himself from my nerves for the rest of my life—(*Ibid.*, p. 209)

---

* How peculiarly apt here seems the statement of Wilhelm Reich:

> . . . The process of armouring in early childhood makes every living expression edgy, mechanical, rigid, incapable of change and adaptation to living functions and processes. The living organ sensations, which have become inaccessible to self-perception, will, from now on, constitute the total realm of ideas which centre around the "SUPERNATURAL." This, too, is tragically logical. Life is beyond reach, "transcendental." Thus it becomes the centre of religious longing for the saviour, the redeemer, the BEYOND. (*Ether, God, and Devil*, pp. 100–101, quoted in Higgins and Raphael, 1968, p. 82)

Reich is speaking here about people in Western society generally.

51

The son thinks the "miracles" are enacted upon objective anatomical organs of his body. He does not see that he is *reenacting* his father's behavior toward his body.

Schreber suffers from reminiscences. His body embodies his past. He retains memories of what his father did to him as a child; although part of his mind knows they are memories, "he" does not. He is considered insane not only because of the quality of his experiences, but because he misconstrues their *mode:* he *remembers,* in some cases perfectly accurately, how his father treated him, but thinks he *perceives* events occurring in the present for which he imagines God, rays, little men, etc., are the agents. (I am speaking loosely when I say he remembers; one is remembering events from one's past, in the strict sense, only if, in reexperiencing them one believes they refer to the past.) In the idiom of David Hume, the eighteenth-century English philosopher, the son experiences "ideas," but thinks he experiences "impressions."

Schreber knows what he most needs to know, but does not know he knows it. When he calls his experiences miracles he denies what he knows, denies he is denying anything, and denies there is anything to deny, *and* he denies those denials too. His "forgetting" here, as in the case of his "forgetting" his father's punishment board, is not the usual amnesia for events of early childhood; his father used belts across the chests of sleeping children starting at seven or eight years old, and the *Geradhalter* and *Kopfhalter* with seven- to sixteen-year-olds.

It is as if Schreber is forbidden by a rule to see the role his father has played in his suffering, and is forbidden by another rule to see that there is anything he does not see, and as if a rule forbids him to see that rule, or *that* a rule might exist. For instance, he never says he cannot find what his experiences mean, and that he cannot because a rule stops him, or that he cannot, and does not know why he cannot. He is certain he knows what they mean; although he discusses their meaning in detail, he never connects them with his father.

The use of one's mind to try to understand the meaning of what one's mind experiences can be uniquely problematic. Ross Ashby in *An Introduction to Cybernetics* (1956) said that when a man cannot see some of the variables of a system, the "system" represented by the remainder may develop remarkable, even *miraculous*, properties (p. 114). A mind observing itself is both observer and system observed; the variables it cannot see may be those it does not *wish* to see, whether or not it knows of its wish. Experiences that arise from a region of one's mind of which one is not ordinarily aware may appear to have extraordinary sources and qualities.

Why did Schreber turn memories into "miracles"? My hypothesis is that he did because his father had forbidden him to see the truth about his past. His father had demanded that children love, honor, and obey their parents. As I illustrate later, he taught parents a method explicitly designed to force children not to feel bitterness or anger toward their parents, even when the feelings might be justified. He wished to rid children of such "dangerous" feelings. Schreber, in order to link his suffering with his father, would have had to consider his father's behavior toward him as "bad." This, I infer, his father had forbidden him to do. He is unable, or unwilling, to violate his father's view of what his view of his father should be. Prohibited from seeing the true origin of his torments, he calls them miracles. Similarly, forbidden from remembering his father's punishment board as such, he reexperiences it as God's "writing-down system." As a result, he is considered crazy.

Over and over again the son says he harbors no "personal grievance" against anyone, intends no "reproach," means not to "recriminate about the past," feels "no ill-will against any human being for what happened in times gone by," wishes to raise no "complaints about the past," etc. (See, for instance, *Memoirs*, pp. 33, 161, 298, and 302.) It is as if he keeps reminding himself and others that he is not feeling what he would like to feel, but cannot feel, about his past.

53

Insofar as he returns in his "nervous illness" to patterns of experience and relation earlier in his life (albeit he denies he is), he can be said in current clinical usage to be regressing. But in so doing he is also partially *undoing repression.* I believe much of what is called regression has as its aim an undoing of repression. It would be important to know how and why Schreber *stopped* repressing and started reexperiencing after forty the suffering of his childhood, albeit he did not know he was remembering it.

> The discourse of the unconscious is structured like a language.
>
> Jacques Lacan

What of the "rays," "little men," and Schreber's other hallucinated persecutors? I presume Schreber needs or wishes to think that the belief signified by the sentence "my father persecuted me" is false and tries to prove it by hallucinating agents other than his father as his persecutors. Images, Sartre has said, are defined by their intentions. I suggest that Schreber invents images in order to contrive evidence to refute the statement "my father persecuted me."

Schreber's hallucinated persecutors and his (repressed) memory-images of his father's persecution both refer, I think, to the same facts: his father's acts of persecution. Memory-images of his father persecuting him would correspond wholly to the facts; the hallucinated images do not.

Suppose one presents oneself (or is presented) with the proposition signified by the sentence "my parent persecuted me," and one wishes or needs to deny its validity. One could refute either the (1) subject, (2) verb, or (3) object of the sentence and say:

My parent did not persecute me:

(1) *someone else* persecuted me.
(2) my parent *freed, helped, loved,* etc., me.
(3) my parent persecuted *someone else.*

Let us assume that memory-images of one's parent's persecution of oneself threaten to parade upon the screen of one's conscious mind and that one wishes or needs to deny their validity. One could form images corresponding to each sentence, (1), (2), or (3), as alternatives to the memory-images.

Images ("image-propositions" in Bertrand Russell's idiom) are necessarily positive; i.e., we can furnish images to portray propositions signified by positive sentences only. We can imagine a man tying a device to a boy's head. We can change the subject, for instance, of the sentence "a man is tying a device to a boy's head" so it reads "little men are tying a device to a boy's head" and conceive an image picturing the new sentence. But we can supply no image of the bare negatives "*no one* is tying a device to a boy's head," "a man is *not tying* a device to a boy's head," or "a man is tying a device to *nothing*."

Schreber, I believe, fashions images of propositions signified by transforms of the sentence "my father persecuted me": he deletes the subject ("my father") and substitutes other subjects ("little men," "rays," "souls," "God," etc.). He could have altered the verb and built images of his father displaying affection (for instance) toward him, but we have no evidence that he did. I have known several people, not regarded as paranoid, whose parents, in my view, persecuted them, who recall repeatedly (or imagine they recall) a parent enacting toward them their, the offsprings', view of love. Possibly, they are replacing the verb in the sentence "my parent persecuted me" so that it reads "my parent loved me." They may be disavowing their experience of their parents no less than Schreber, but no term exists in English or psychiatric usage to describe them; perhaps this is why they have gone unrecognized. I have known too a few persons, considered paranoid, whose parents I also think persecuted them, who shape images based, it seems, on an exchange both of the subject *and* verb of the sentence "my parent persecuted me": they form images, as Schreber does, of agents other than their parents persecuting them, *and* recall (or imagine they

55

recall) memory-images of a parent treating them, in the off-springs' view, lovingly.

In theory, Schreber could also have distorted the object in the sentence "my father persecuted me" and imagined or "remembered" his father persecuting *someone else;* apparently he did not. I can think of no clear-cut example of this type of substitution occurring in isolation. Possibly, anyone who feels forbidden to think of a parent persecuting him feels forbidden to think of the parent persecuting anyone. Many persons change, I believe, both subject and object of the proposition signified by the sentence "my parent persecuted me." For instance, in dreams or while masturbating, they imagine an older person, not their parent, beating or otherwise persecuting a child, not them. I regard this image as a double replacement for the image-proposition, "my parent beat (or persecuted) me."

Suppose an event occurs in one's mind in the presence of a preexistent rule forbidding the event. The event could later form the basis for a hallucination if one followed this formula:

Construct a sentence to render the event in words.

Withdraw consciousness from the event.

Deny the previous steps, the next steps,
and the denials.

Change the subject, verb, or object of the
sentence and form a new positive sentence.

Picture the new sentence with an image.

Project the image into perceptual space.

Of course, hallucinations, like dreams, do not say about themselves that they have come into being as products of operations upon past experiences. The hallucinator, I think, denies those experiences and the operations he performs upon them.

It may be because we write, read, speak, and hear words in

linear succession, each word and sentence before or after another, that we sometimes suppose our "line" of thinking follows a sequence, logical or otherwise. When we describe a course of thinking we presume it progresses along steps of some sort, each step dependent on prior ones. Our view of how we think may not correspond to how, in fact, we think. In the foregoing formula the last step needs to happen sometime after the first, but all the others could occur in any sequence, or all at once, at any time during the interval between the first step and the last.

To hallucinate regularly one might apply this formula to a set of events which occurred regularly in one's past. This may not be the only method for forming hallucinations, but it seems to me it may be a frequently used one.*

One can also use ordinary perceptions and memories to replace and stand for perceptions and memories that are forbidden to awareness. One Jewish man I know, whenever he sees or hears, or remembers seeing or hearing, references in conversation or the mass media to Nazis, Germans, blond-haired, or handsome men, draws support from these experiences for his oft-repeated belief that Nazis persecute or persecuted Jews or that Nazis persecute or persecuted him. He has never met a genuine Nazi; his father, in my view, persecutes him. I regard his focus upon these particular perceptions and memories and his constructions upon them as substitutes for perceptions and memories of his father's persecution of him. Perception, like memory, is partly a moral choice.

If one connects in this way one's feelings of persecution with

---

* In order to hallucinate regularly one only needs practice. What is called a hallucination can be considered a form of thinking; so can a dream, as Freud said. The ability to think with images while awake is more prevalent in children than adults, at least in our society. Many creative people retain the ability; most people do not, probably owing to the general view that such experiences are undesirable or "sick." To regain the ability, it is simply necessary to disinhibit the block.

ordinary perceptions or memories, one is likely to be considered, in psychiatric idiom, deluded, not hallucinated. Of course, one can both invent new perceptive experiences (hallucinations) and adapt ordinary ones and memories for one's purposes: one can be seen as both hallucinated and deluded.*

What is called a hallucination or a delusion may be a mind's attempt to reveal itself to itself, given the presence of a rule it imposes upon itself that forbids it to do just that. Without the rule, it might not need the hallucination or delusion.

The word "hallucinate" derives from the past participle stem of the Latin *(h)allucinari*, to wander in mind, to talk idly. If my formula fits some hallucinators, their minds are not wandering, but are moving along carefully charted paths with clear aims. Nor are they speaking idly; they may be revealing, albeit in code, the core of their being.

I have suggested that hallucinations may be *picturing* propositions that could also be signified by sentences. Could the patterns of spoken or written language in a given culture, subculture, or family influence the hallucinations or dreams of its members? Language patterns may govern *all* perceptive experience including ordinary perceptions (see Whorf, 1964). Consider, for instance, how differently we might experience the world and ourselves if the grammar of our language did not

---

* Certain features of my hypothesis formally resemble von Domarus' (1964) view of "paralogical" thinking, which he believes characterizes schizophrenic thought. Von Domarus says paralogical thinking accepts identity based on identical predicates. He says:
  If A means "certain Indians are swift" and B means "stags are swift" the area of intersection of A and B symbolises the common element of swiftness.
  It follows for the paralogical thinker that "Certain Indians are stags," and he will act as his conclusion directs him to do. (p. 110)
To clarify the differences and similarities between von Domarus' view and my position here would require a few pages and would take us off our course. His theory offers no motive or intent for paralogical thinking. Similarly, Bleuler fails to consider that persons whose thinking he finds peculiar might have motives or intents for thinking as they do.

require sentences to have subjects and if therefore we did not presume actions need agents or subjects.

> "The light flashed" we say in English. Something has to be there to make the flash; "light" is the subject, "flash" the predicate. . . . A Hopi Indian says *Reh-pi*—"flash"—one word for the whole performance, no subject, no predicate, no time element. We frequently read into nature *ghostly entities* which flash and *perform other miracles*. Do we supply them because some of our verbs require substantives in front of them? (Foreword by Stuart Chase in Whorf, 1964, p. viii)

If my theory of Schreber's hallucinations is right, were he a Hopi, he might not have needed to create ghostly performers of "miracles" to be agents of his persecution; he might have re-experienced feelings of persecution without inventing imaginary persecutors.

To hallucinate is to situate images in perceptual space. Seeing (or hearing, touching, smelling, tasting, etc.) is believing. Sensory experience is proverbially the least open to question; it is self-evident. So the man in the street thinks, physicists, psychologists, and philosophers notwithstanding. Hallucinations seem real to those who have them, often more compellingly real than other perceptive experiences. Hallucinators do not yield to arguments; the immediacy of their experience allows no doubts.

Schreber says in a postscript to his *Memoirs*, "Concerning Hallucinations":

> By hallucinations one understands, as far as I know, stimulation of nerves by virtue of which a person with a nervous illness believes he has impressions of events in the external world . . . which in reality do not exist. Science seems to deny any reality background for hallucinations, judging from what I have read for instance in Kraepelin. . . . In my opinion this is definitely erroneous, at least if so generalised. . . . Serious doubts in such a rationalistic and purely materialistic (if I may say so) attitude must arise in cases where one is dealing with voices of "supernatural origin." . . . I can of course only speak with cer-

59

tainty of myself when I maintain that an external cause for these sensations exists. (p. 223)

Schreber, it seems, gives himself perceptive experience in order to support his wish to *dis*believe his father's persecution of him. It is as if he is saying: "memory-images of my father do not persecute me; supernatural powers do." Of course, to affirm something to oneself does not prove its truth. Evidence about events one experiences as originating outside one's skin is eligible to be regarded as valid only if others can experience it too. In the West, someone who derives conclusions from perceptive experience he invents in order to prove or disprove his beliefs is liable to be seen as insane or unscientific, depending upon the context. He is breaking basic rules.

Schreber was labeled insane and would be today. What of his father? The father, starting from false premises about children's physical and psychological needs, inferred how parents should treat children, and treated his son strangely. The son suffered his father's conduct, later reexperienced it (without realizing it), and drew inferences from his reexperiences, which in turn led him to false conclusions about the spiritual order of the cosmos.

FATHER	SON
false premises	false conclusions
↓	↑
inferences	inferences
↓	↑
strange behavior_ _ _ _ _ _ ►	strange experience

If the test of a mind's soundness were its knowledge of truth about itself, other minds, or the world, I should find it hard to decide who in this case is madder, father or son. It is whimsical to view the son as deranged and the father as sane and worthy of high esteem.

Schreber's hospital records (Baumeyer, 1956) and Weber's report (Postscript to *Memoirs*) reveal that his doctors regarded

60

his lack of insight into his illness as a symptom of his illness. But I see no evidence that they had more understanding than he of his experiences. Nor would many mental hospital doctors today; their view that paranoia and schizophrenia arise from events whose origins lie only within the "ill" individuals would *interfere* with their understanding Schreber.

Schreber, although he does not explicitly connect his father's behavior with events of his "nervous illness," occasionally hints at links. For instance, he accuses Dr. Flechsig, his first hospital doctor:

> You, *like so many doctors,* could not completely resist the temptation of using a patient . . . as an object for . . . experiments. (*Memoirs,* p. 34)

The psychiatrists who treated Schreber did not even come this close to the truth about his relation with his father. Schreber says Dr. Flechsig

> wanted to put down my illness solely [!] to poisoning with potassium bromide, for which Dr. R. in S., in whose care I had been before, was to be blamed. (*Ibid.,* p. 62)

And Dr. Weber, a later psychiatrist, says Schreber's "miracles" are "undoubtedly due to pathological processes of the brain" (Postscript to *Memoirs,* p. 320).

Apparently, it never occurred to Flechsig, Weber, or any other doctor who treated Schreber or who in the next fifty years wrote about him to link Schreber's suffering with his father's behavior. Possibly, even if Schreber could have laid bare for all to see how his "miracles" were memories, he might have found no one ready to understand.

NATURE AND UNNATURE

In my case, moral obliquity lay in God placing Himself
outside the Order of the World by which He Himself must
be guided; . . .

Daniel Paul Schreber, *Memoirs,* p. 78

Certain persons, including Dr. Schreber, Daniel Paul's father, consider and call their moral ideals laws of nature. They suppose acts, thoughts, and relationships that match their moral ideals are natural and those that do not are unnatural. They claim thereby the authority of universality for their own ideals, however parochial and ethnocentric. Many people regard most forms of sexual relationship between human beings as unnatural: oral-genital sex, relations between more than two persons at once, between two persons of the same sex or of different color, etc.

Perhaps it is necessary that men choose moral ideals of some sort. But to see one's own choices as natural and others as unnatural is to deny that one's moral ideals are partly contingent upon one's programming, which in turn is influenced by one's social contexts, past and present.

A preeminent goal of Dr. Schreber's system of education is

that man bring his "sophisticated world" into "harmony with the all-governing *laws of Nature* and the Order of the World" (1858, p. 308).

> An education according to Reason and Nature should deduce from these prime principles all specific and directly practical principles and bring them into prime connection with these. (*Ibid.*, p. 27)

He urges his readers to "obey" Nature. He says about "our school system":

> All major shortcomings stem from the fact that not all laws and institutions are based on the *laws of Nature*, and that even more so the individual teacher does not use them as a guide of conduct. (p. 308)

He rails against "excesses of all kinds," which he calls an unnatural mode of life (p. 235).

Moral laws, not laws of Nature, define what men think *ought* to occur: Nature (or the Order of the World) defines what *must* happen. What is really unnatural does not and could not take place. If what Dr. Schreber calls Nature really were Nature, he would not need to urge readers to "obey" it, since they could not choose not to. All that actually comes to pass within and between persons is, in some sense, natural. But he does not see this.

His son makes the same mistake; he regards what he considers moral as natural, and immoral as unnatural:

> The whole idea of morality can arise only within the Order of the World, that is to say within the natural bond which holds God and mankind together; wherever the Order of the World is broken, power alone counts, and the right of the stronger is decisive. In my case, moral obliquity lay in God placing Himself outside the Order of the World by which He Himself must be guided. . . . (*Memoirs*, p. 78)

Here the son criticizes God's (read father's) maltreatment of him, but not his father's premise about the relationship between morality and the Order of the World.

Dr. Schreber, the father, thinks that what are, in fact, his prejudices are "fixed in nature":

> It is fixed in nature that the rearing of a boy is as a rule considerably more difficult and requires a higher degree of energy than that of a girl. (1858, p. 165)

"Explanatory advice" about the "danger of lust" (which he sees as "unnatural passion") must be

> both more detailed and more weighty when it concerns boys than where girls are involved. (*Ibid.*, p. 251)

His sons may have turned out as they did *because* of the greater "energy" he probably devoted to their rearing.

He deploys Nature to mean whatever he wishes: he refers to the "*unnatural* pressure towards full emancipation of the schools from the Church" (1860, p. 17). Despite the lack of a shred of scientific evidence to support his moral and most of his pseudo-medical precepts, he contrasts the "crude empiricism" of past centuries with his own presumably superior learning from "life itself," from the "Book of Nature."

Dr. Schreber alleges his other overall aim is that persons

> reach that moral height which is the crown of Christian *moral law*. (1858, p. 288)

He wishes to escort the child

> towards full noble warmth of feeling and the purest love in the *Christian* sense. (*Ibid.*, p. 26)

He sees no conflict, actual or potential, between Christian moral law and what he calls Nature and the Order of the World. What he regards as morally right *is* what he considers natural. Moral rules are so deeply implanted in him that he sees violations of them as unnatural.

Dr. Schreber thinks he applies Christian moral law (as he understands it) to the education of children and that he does it *scientifically*. The theory and methods of what is called social science can be used to study Christian moral law (however understood or applied) as one of innumerable actual or possible systems of moral law. But this is not what he means by science. He believes his application of Christian moral law to the upbringing of children is a science. The "science of education," to which he thinks his system belongs, is

> one of the foremost and abundant sciences amongst its intellectual sisters. (p. 24)

He deplores the fact that

> not one university has set up a special chair in it. (p. 24)

When he pretends his moral precepts are scientifically valid, he makes it hard, since he is a doctor, for children and most laymen to challenge his authority. Few laymen even today see that doctors often confuse morals with science. Much theory and practice of psychiatry today is based on precisely such confusion.*

Dr. Schreber asserts that he obeys "the laws of Nature," but in fact he *opposes* Nature:

> The noble seeds of human nature sprout in their purity almost upwards by themselves if the ignoble ones (the weeds) are sought out and uprooted in time. This must be done ruthlessly and with vigour. (p. 140)

---

* I have elaborated upon this issue previously (Schatzman, 1970). Here, briefly, is the nub of the argument:

> The tradition of scientific medicine teaches a doctor to keep distinct his moral attitude toward diseased persons from his nonmoral objective attitude toward their diseases. But the *moral* views of the psychiatrist and his society define what persons he sees, labels, and treats as mentally ill; he sees certain "unnatural" acts, such as homosexuality, as mental illnesses. Especially if he works in a mental hospital, he is concerned with surveying morals and mediating rules. He talks about his work, however, with terms borrowed from the disease model: "symptom," "treatment," "remission," "cure," etc.

> The separation of each single branch or leaf from the weed is
> an important gain for life. (p. 162)

Botanically, weeds belong to no species in particular; they are
any plants which grow where a gardener does not wish them
to grow. Just as weeds exist in the eye of the gardener, so Dr.
Schreber defines for himself the "weeds" of which he speaks.
Both real weeds and the "weeds" Dr. Schreber means are natural growths. How can Dr. Schreber align himself with Nature
while calling for "uprooting" of weeds?

He severely suppresses natural (in the sense of unrestrained)
body posture and movements, natural eating habits, natural sexuality, etc. For instance, children must not eat between meals:

> The inevitable consequence is incomplete and ill blood forma-
> tion. This widespread mistake in child-rearing should be seen as
> the root cause of the sickliness and feebleness of our youth.
> (p. 166)

Medically this is nonsense. But he seems to feel he must but-
tress his case, as in his discussions of body posture and sexuality,
with the *appearance* of medical fact.

He also opposes children eating between meals for a moral
reason: they must learn "self-denial." He could be sadistic in
pursuing his high-minded goals. Consider this regimen to train
a child, before the age of *one*, in "self-denial." No one must give
the infant a morsel of food besides the regular three meals a
day. His nurse seats him on her lap while she eats or drinks
whatever she wishes. However much the child should wish food
or drink, she must give him none.

> A child so trained will sit calmly and cheerfully playing or
> dallying on the lap of his attendant, who is eating, without
> bothering the slightest about this . . . Be concerned to maintain
> the child in solid, good habits by frequently making use of such
> opportunities. Whether the persons charged with attending the
> child have been scrupulous enough will be unfailingly borne out
> by the child's behaviour. As soon as a child displays a desire

caused by something or other and quite out of place, one may certainly assume that weakness towards the child has been shown on someone's part. I have reached this conviction from sufficient personal experience. And even if such an infringement has only happened once (perhaps secretly on the part of the nurse), this will certainly become apparent at the next opportunity through the child's behaviour: it wants to have. Therefore one should not fear accusing without reason the child's immediate surroundings, which can thus be easily and surely controlled. As far as this goes a child can never deceive us. (p. 64)

He adds:

Here is only a small experience from my own family circle. The nurse of one of my children, generally a very sweet person, once gave a child something between his meals even though having been told explicitly not to. . . . It was a piece of pear which she herself was eating. . . . She was without any other reason dismissed from the service at once because I had lost the necessary trust in her unconditional correctness. (p. 64n)

News about the episode spread among the children's nurses in Leipzig and from then on, he says, he had "no further trouble with any other such erring maids or nurses."

Dr. Schreber's method of teaching a baby self-denial is to set up a hierarchy by which he applies his power upon the nurse to apply hers upon the baby. Only the baby is denied anything. It is relevant that the son in his "nervous illness" many years later experienced "a hierarchy of powers in the realm of God." He may have been reexperiencing the hierarchy of powers in the realm of his father.

The father specifies in detail what children up to seven years should eat and drink at each meal, what they must never eat or drink, when they are and are not allowed to drink water, and how often and at what times meals should be. He offers a potpourri of moral and pseudomedical reasons for his rules: "correct blood formation," "moral considerations," right "diluting" of "digestive juices," "protection against excess (and there-

fore the preponderance of animal functions over the spiritual),"
right "degree of metabolism," "the consistency of order,"
avoidance of a "pampered stomach," and the attainment by the
"digestive system" of "full strength" (pp. 74–77 and p. 166).

It is "weak" to give in to the child's tastes or whims (p. 76).
If a child does not wish to eat offered food, one must see "most
strictly" to its "uncurtailed consumption" by the child.

> At the first instance of such whims one should *never* give in;
> one should not give the child a morsel of anything else until he
> has *completely* eaten the refused food. . . . After a few firm ap-
> plications of this maxim nothing of this sort will ever occur to
> the child again. Here too the proverb proves true: a stitch in
> time saves nine. (pp. 76–77)

In this way one sees to it that the child is not

> burdened with a load of peculiarities which are of a manifold
> inhibiting influence in his later life. (p. 77)

Strict parental control of what and when children eat and
drink must continue until seventeen, and the "partaking of
exotic stimulating food" is forbidden before twenty (p. 278).
Exercises in posture ("the shoulders should be thrust back and
the back held rigid") should be done regularly twice a day, for
ten to fifteen minutes before breakfast and supper. This is a
guard against "disorderliness and forgetfulness" and is a "good
way of making the child remember":

> Whether he gets his meal or not will be determined by
> whether he has carried out his posture exercises. (p. 209)

The father demands that a child *dis*obey the child's natural
desires to eat. The son may be reexperiencing his father's assaults against his appetite when he says:

> For a time the miracles were in preference directed against my
> stomach, partly because the souls begrudged me the sensual
> pleasure connected with the taking of food, partly because they
> considered themselves superior to human beings who require

69

earthly nourishments; they therefore tended to look down on all eating and drinking with disdain. (*Memoirs*, p. 133)

In order to meet the demands of the father's system, a child would have to learn to ignore and to forget he was ignoring all signals of hunger (and some of satiety) from his digestive tract. In effect, he would have to forget, especially between meals, he had a stomach. Schreber says:

> I existed frequently without a stomach; I expressly told the attendant . . . that I could not eat because I had no stomach. Sometimes immediately before meals a stomach was so to speak produced *ad hoc* by miracles. (*Ibid.*, pp. 133–134)

He also spoke of his bowels having disappeared "in a mysterious way" (Baumeyer, 1956, p. 65).

Where Dr. Schreber allows children to be natural it is in order to "scrutinise" them and to make it easier to impose his views upon them, i.e., to undermine their naturalness:

> When the child is among his playmates, his full natural individuality is at its clearest prominence. The unselfconsciousness and lack of inhibition involved opens every fold, even the deepest, of his inner life. It is here that the child can be most completely *scrutinised*. . . . Parents and educators . . . find in this a very fruitful means for observation and for establishing their educational standpoint. (1858, p. 120)

He says:

> The following may be considered as a first educational rule with regard to children's games: choose exclusively those games which give the greatest free rein to the child's spontaneity within the bounds of what is allowed. (*Ibid.*, p. 112)

Note the qualifications he places upon the child's "spontaneity": parents (1) choose the games, (2) determine what is allowed, (3) decide if a given game is "within the bounds of what is allowed." In this context, talk of "giving free rein to the child's spontaneity" is a mystification. He suggests other restraints:

One must seek to introduce the correct balance and alternation in accordance with the child's temperament between games involving movement and quiet games.

Thus a number of unsatisfactory and extreme traits of the child's individuality, which are difficult to smooth out at a later stage, can now be easily controlled. (p. 113)

Thus, parents should decide (4) which are "quiet" games and which are not, (5) which "traits" are "unsatisfactory and extreme," (6) what is "the child's temperament," and (7) what the "correct balance" between games is that "accords" with it. Similarly, children's play with toys is under parents' control.

Do not allow the child to occupy himself with more than one toy at any time. . . . Pay heed that the change is made only after the child has used sufficient energy (physical or mental) on the given toy. . . . Above all, toys offer the opportunity of turning cleanliness, care for property, and tidiness into firm rules. (p. 115)

In short, children's play gives parents a chance to manipulate children. Perhaps it is to this the son refers when he speaks of being the victim of the "cursed" "play-with-human-beings [*Menschenspielerei*]" (*Memoirs*, p. 94).

Parents, not children, pick the dramas, if any, their children can see:

Simply as a superficial means of amusement or entertainment, plays, such as heroic or tragic ones, are hardly advisable pleasures, and they should be allowed on very limited occasions and after extremely careful choice. (1858, p. 259)

He never says why plays are "hardly advisable pleasures." Maybe he thought he was protecting children's "mental stability":

An immoderate indulgence in the pleasures of art, or too exclusive involvement in life in an artistic sphere, finally exhausts the nervous system, produces an unhealthy sensitivity, hypo-

71

chondria, hysteria, fantasies, and takes away the physical and mental stability. (*Ibid.*, pp. 292–293)

Ironically, his son's doctors thought he suffered from precisely the conditions the father meant to prevent.

Dr. Schreber also dictates rules about children's baths: the temperature of the water at each age, the number of inches of water in the tub, the number of minutes they must spend in it, and, in the summer, the number of minutes outdoors before entering the tub (pp. 80–81). He specifies how many hours a day children under twelve must spend outdoors in each season. Should "circumstances" reduce the hours one day, they must spend more hours the next day. The child's preferences in these matters are irrelevant.

I have already mentioned Dr. Schreber's fear of damage to a child who lies too long on one side. Warnings against "one-sidedness" abound in his writings. He uses the term "one-sidedness" to refer to the development by one side of the body, right or left, of greater strength than the other. He intervened to a remarkable extent in children's lives in order to prevent it. Needless to say, his alarms lack scientific validity. If an infant learning to walk is being led by a hand:

> an even alternation of right and left must always be adhered to, since the arm and shoulder muscles of the child are in increased activity on the side that is grasped. . . . Unevenness in the habituation and development of both sides of the body would result if the alternation were omitted. (p. 85)

In a section called "Body Form, Carriage, and Habits" he says about children one to seven years old:

> An unusually bad habit is standing on one foot whereby the other hangs and only touches the floor lightly and the whole upper part of the body is put into a slack and uneven deportment. . . . The horizontal position of the hips is upset since the side on which the body weight rests is forced upwards while the other side hangs down. This causes an S-bend to one side of

72

the spine, which results in a dislodged uneven carriage of the whole upper part of the body. . . . Only through consequent and, if required, severe reprimanding can this bad habit be controlled.

When climbing [or descending] stairs . . . children under 6–7 years are unable to overstep due to their short legs, but are forced to pull one leg behind the other, step by step. Most children are used to doing this in one and the same way without alternating each leg. . . . It can be the cause of uneven formation of the frail and yielding body of the child . . . One should take care that the child uses both legs alternately when climbing stairs. (pp. 101–102)

He takes three full pages to explain the general principle. A few sentences give the gist of it:

It is of great importance that the limbs of the child's body should develop and be trained totally equally. (p. 102. He italicizes the whole passage.)

In order to comply with this consideration—which is of great practical advantage as far as health and future occupation is concerned—it is important that neither side of the body is neglected, no arm or leg stays behind in any movement or occupation. . . . The child must learn that everything it does with one arm or leg it must do with the other, regularly alternating. (pp. 102–103. He italicizes this last sentence.)

"Special attention" must be paid to see to it that a child one to seven years old uses both hands alternately to pick up and carry things. The same is so for

reaching up . . . onto door knobs (which are designed for the height of adults), which causes lifting of the arm and shoulder and a stretching of this whole side of the body. (p. 105)

"Alternating between the left and right is necessary" in games:

especially ball-, whirligig-, and dice-games, [which] are subject to one-sided muscle activities. . . . Girls should carry their dolls on the right as well as with the left hand. (pp. 105–106)

He makes the next few statements in a section on seven to sixteen year olds:

> Swimming on one side . . . is particularly inadvisable. (p. 171)

He warns against "sitting awkwardly (to one side)":

> In this, one elbow rests on the table whilst the other hangs down. Always associated with this is a greater or lesser contortion of the trunk, and on closer inspection of a child sitting this way one will always find that one shoulder is lower than the other. . . . This defective habit is one of the most frequent causes . . . of the formation of spinal curving to one side. (p. 200)

He prohibits writing while standing:

> almost always they only stand on one foot at a time because a need for relaxation forces the feet to this. (p. 202)

He forbids most musical instruments to avoid one-sidedness:

> Even playing the clarinet, horn, or oboe could count as harmful in this sense if it were not already excluded for children by virtue of the effort involved for the lungs. On the other hand, playing any string instrument (including harp, flute, zither, and guitar) is obviously bad for the child's physical posture and development. (p. 211)

For the same reason he discourages

> carrying smaller children in one's arms, carrying heavy satchels, carrying water-cans, etc. (p. 212)

He debars

> drawing and painting at an easel, due to considerable unequalness in shoulder positioning, and because all alternation is not really possible. (p. 213)

In order to prevent "one-sidedness" in girls, he objects to the usual design of petticoats:

> It is unavoidable that the laces, which are often tied carelessly and unequally above the hips, are pulled down by the weight of

the skirts and cut in more on one side than the other, causing the endeavour to pull in one of the hips. (p. 192)

He says about sewing, embroidery, and hair-plaiting:

> In addition to the fact that in these, as in all occupations involving sitting, curving the back should be avoided, one should also remember that sewing with a long thread is unsuitable for young girls, on account of the regular raising of the arm and shoulder on one side, which can easily lead to a deformity of the shoulder. For the same reason frame-embroidering is quite unsuited for girls. (p. 212)
>
> Girls plaiting their hair must do this alternately on both right and left sides. (p. 213)

He gives many more examples, often accompanied by orthopedic pseudoclarifications. He says he does not mean them to compose an exhaustive list, but to illustrate the proper principles and to serve as "guidelines" for *all* activities.

A hospital report (Baumeyer, 1956) about the son's conduct later on says:

> His posture and gait are rigid, his movements stiff and angular. (p. 65)

Maybe he was trying to avoid "slack and uneven deportment," "curving of the back," unequalness in shoulder positioning," "an S-bend to one side of the spine," "one-sidedness of his limb muscles," etc., all at once.

It is amusing to note how the son could thwart his father's ends. Dr. Weber, writing in 1902 when the son was sixty, refers to the "extraordinary position" of his head (Postcript to *Memoirs*, p. 324). Baumeyer (1970) recently met a seventy-nine-year-old woman who had been adopted at thirteen by the son's wife and had lived with him during the time he was out of the hospital from 1903 to 1907; she said he *always* held his head to one side. Was this a belated defiance and mockery of his father's aims?

As we have seen, "one-sidedness" is not the only type of physical malformation, a fear of which leads the father to limit children's activities, nor is anxiety over bodily maldevelopment the only reason he restricts children's movements. It seems that almost any move a child could make from birth to adult life would come under one of his constraints. It would either have to be "balanced" by the same move with the opposite side of the body or be forbidden. Under the circumstances his own child might have thought it simpler not to move at all sometimes.

For part of the time Schreber was in mental hospital this is exactly what he did; he says:

> My outward life was extremely monotonous during that time—the first months of my stay at Sonnenstein. Apart from daily morning and afternoon walks in the garden I sat *motionless* the whole day on a chair at my table. . . ; even in the garden I preferred to remain seated always in the same spot. (*Memoirs*, p. 127; italics in original)

His motionlessness can be seen as a transform of a position he might have, as a child, either adopted or feared not to adopt.

Dr. Weber says Schreber "sat for hours completely stiff and immobile." (Postscript to *Memoirs*, pp. 267–268). Weber does not see that Schreber's behavior could be intelligible in terms of his upbringing, or in any psychological terms; he calls it a hallucinatory stupor. Schreber's father had prohibited not only sitting to one side, but sitting with "compressed chest," with "the upper body bent a long way forward and the head hanging down," and with legs crossed (due to "checks in blood flow and other delicate reasons") (1858, p. 200). The son's "stiff and immobile" sitting could be an attempt, or a memory of an attempt, to *adapt* to a set of injunctions designed to govern nearly all his postures and movements.

Schreber says about his immobility:

I kept it up myself for a time until I realised it was purposeless.

He says he is "convinced" it must "be connected"

with God not knowing how to treat a living human being,

and with God's

more or less absurd ideas, which were all *contrary* to human nature. (*Memoirs*, p. 127)

SEX: FATHER
AND SON

> Few people have been brought up according to such
> strict moral principles as I, and have throughout life
> practised such moderation especially in matters of sex,
> as I venture to claim for myself.
>
> Daniel Paul Schreber, *Memoirs*, p. 208

To be free means to lack constraints. No one's behavior or experience is random; everyone is partly unfree. But persons are
constrained to varying degrees. Only a few freedoms may be
constrained or many may be. When people call someone rigid,
inhibited, constricted, fixated, up-tight, etc., they usually mean
they think he shrinks from possibilities of experience and behavior in which they indulge.

Note someone's behavior. Envisage a set of possibilities wider
than this person displays. Why is his actual behavior restricted
to some part of the possible? Why these limits and not others?
What and where are the constraints and what is their origin?

A constraint is a type of relation between two sets. When
variety in an observable set is smaller than variety in a possible
set, a constraint is present. Constraints make a set smaller than
it might be. The larger set would be present if the constraints

were not. It is theoretically possible (though in practice, virtually impossible) to specify all the constraints governing someone in a given situation. The more constraints, the fewer options, the less flexibility.

Individuals who receive psychiatric diagnoses are usually severely constrained. Among their constraints are some that prevent them from avoiding or seeing how to avoid allowing themselves to be in a situation in which a psychiatrist could label them.

A phobic is so called because he suffers from a constraint whereby he cannot for instance enter an elevator or subway without feeling fear. A "sexual pervert" is so called not just because of his sexual acts or interests, but because he is thought to be constrained not to make genital heterosexual love. It is less often appreciated that someone labeled schizophrenic or paranoid can be seen to be rigorously constrained. A clinical report about such a person generally inventories what he says and does, nearly never what he fails to say and do. Someone may speak "schizophrenese" because he does not feel permitted to say what he has to say plainly and directly.

Much of Schreber's so-called madness can be seen to be the result of an accumulation of his adaptations to his father's constraints. I have already shown how he may have suffered from a rule forbidding him to identify his father as his persecutor.

Schreber throughout much of his "nervous illness" showed no interest, as far as we know, in ordinary sexual activities or feelings. His doctors never mentioned this omission. Perhaps constraints prevented them from noting that constraints were keeping Schreber's consciousness apart from his sexual feelings. I shall discuss here the possible origin of his celibacy in thought and deed.

The triumph of spirit over matter: Dr. Schreber again and again says his system of child-rearing embodies and can fulfill this goal.

In accordance with the divine idea of the creation of the human race . . . all individual aims should directly or indirectly strive to attain the highest goal: the greatest elevation and strengthening of Christian moral self-awareness that is humanly possible, the continually ascending victory of spiritual nature over the body-nature [*Körper-Natur*], the spiritual enlightenment of the human race. (1860, p. 11)

The law of progress to the better, the nobler, the more perfect, the law of the battle of endeavour towards the divine, the law of the gradual victory of spirit over matter . . . goes through the whole history of the human race as the almighty spirit of God. . . . Each new generation has the task of attaching itself to this stream, visible only to the spiritual eye . . . : not just to be equal to its parents, but to become more perfect, in order to deliver to the subsequent generation an increased inheritance. (*Ibid.*, p. 15)

He writes in the millennial idiom of humanity's most awakened minds. "Spirit over matter" has *also* been a slogan in the mouths of well-meaning self-appointed apostles who would, in the name of God's purity, merely stifle our sex lives.

Dr. Schreber had views about sex which were in tune with the spirit of his time and which today would be seen as strange indeed in many circles, though not in all. He buttressed his views with moral arguments and with ideas about physical and mental health which he mistook for established truths. For instance, he opposes girls' clothes that are "cut so low that they easily slide off the shoulders":

The uncomfortable sensation connected with this causes a continuous unequal raising and moving to and fro of the shoulders and thus easily becomes in the course of time the cause of the origin of permanent incorrect habits and postures. (1858, p. 189)

Speaking of the appearance of "seeds of passion" in seven- to seventeen-year-olds, he says:

We should best apply the general rule here; all ignoble and immoral . . . emotions must be suffocated in their seed right

81

away by immediate diversion or direct suppression. Generally, this basic rule refers to the moral-sensible control of all the physical aspects of sensuality in the widest sense of the word. . . . (*Ibid.*, p. 241)

The son in his *Memoirs* writes:

Decisive for my mental collapse was one particular night; during that night I had a quite unusual number of *pollutions* * (perhaps half a dozen).

From then on appeared the first signs of communication with supernatural powers. . . . (p. 68)

What his father says about "pollutions" sheds light on why a night of "pollutions" was so "decisive" for him. The father thinks "pollutions" are the cause or the effect (it is unclear which) of "nervous overstrain" and "over-tense nerves"; he recommends muscular exercise as "remedy" and "cure." In his book *Medical Indoor Gymnastics*, he says about exercise:

Under medical direction this may become a most important remedy, or, in any case, an indispensable agent for the cure of all cases of muscular paralysis, extreme excitability or dullness of the nervous system, nervous hypochondria and hysteria, *unhealthy enfeebling pollutions,* diseases of the mind, and certain chronic convulsive ailments such as St. Vitus's dance, epilepsy, etc. (1899, p. 9)

In a section called "Prescription for Unhealthy, Weakening, Frequency of Pollutions" (*ibid.*, p. 79) he suggests a regimen of sixteen exercises to prevent "pollutions" or their imagined effects. The exercises must be done four to one hundred times daily, depending on the exercise and how long one has been doing them. They are "arm-circling," "arm-raising sideways," "elbows backwards," "arm-striking forwards," "arm-striking

---

* The son and the father use this term for what are now called wet dreams, i.e., emissions of semen in sleep. To call them pollutions, meaning impurity and defilement, is to presuppose their harmfulness.

outwards," "arm-striking upwards," "sawing movement," "striking the arms together," "throwing the arms apart," "sitting down," "mowing movement," "hand rubbing," "hewing movement," "arm waving sideways," and "sawing movement" (again). He illustrates each exercise with a drawing; he specifies whether intervals "for deep breathing" should be taken and if dumbbells may be used. The exercises should not be done "later than before the evening meal," he says. In "persistent" cases,

> It is also advisable before going to bed . . . to take a hip-bath of a temperature between 54° and 60° Fahr. for 6–8 minutes, or a simple water enema of the same temperature which should be retained as long as possible (and therefore not too abundant), and at night, in this case, as an exception, instead of lying on the back, make a habit as an alternative, of lying on the side; and in the morning, not at night, wash the parts around the sexual organs and the perinaeum with cold water. (p. 80; translation amended)

How bizarre the father's behavior is! I wonder what figment of his imagination he was cleansing by enemas and where and how he learned to think enemas could cleanse it.

With these procedures Dr. Schreber turns to *magic* to deal with his fears of "pollution"; he does not see it is magic to which he turns. These rituals could have engendered fears of the effects of "pollutions" in anyone taught to use them.

Certain men compulsively enact ceremonies to ward off anxiety within themselves. Their rites can induce anxiety in others, especially those who witness them as children and are brought up with them. Someone's obsessional practices can *create* a sense of danger in others.

I suggest what may have been "decisive" for the son's "mental collapse" were not the "pollutions" alone, but the view that "pollutions" can be "unhealthy" and "enfeebling." His father's rituals embodied and communicated this view. The father, like others of that era who tried to "cure" "pollutors," did not seem to see that his fear of "pollutions" may have induced in "pollutors" psychological effects of the exact sort the "cures" were meant to prevent.

The father endorses no sort of sexual activity anywhere in his writings. This omission is especially striking in the book *Medical Indoor Gymnastics*, since in it he urges readers, at least in principle, to use their "bodily powers," not to forget "the demands of their physical side," and to "obey" "Nature," who "punishes those who oppose her," often "very sharply." "Those will be wise who understand and obey the first hints of Nature demanding her rights . . ." (p. 16). He mentions sex only once (except for talk of "pollutions") in this ninety-eight-page book —he lists "sexual exhaustion" incorrectly as a cause of the

> ailments of middle life,—the host of chronic ailments of the bowels, hemorrhoidal disorders, stoppages of the blood, signs of gout, asthmatic symptoms, hypochondria, hysteria, melancholy, paralytic symptoms, attacks of apoplexy and so on. (p. 16)

In discussing the value of gymnastics in his *Kallipädie*, he asserts, also incorrectly,

> There is another important special advantage which the pursuit of vigorous physical movement contributes at this age [7–16], and that is the prevention of the premature development of sexual maturity—the result of an indolent, soft, and dissipated life. (1858, p. 177)

He forbids masturbation, sometimes without saying what he forbids, why he forbids it, why he does not say what he forbids, or that there is something he does not say. I suppose he hopes, by not specifying what he forbids, to encourage parents and teachers by his example to find ways to tell a child not to masturbate without explicitly telling him not to; it is easier to suppress someone's behavior if he does not know what is suppressed. But Dr. Schreber does not say this either. He leaves no doubt, however, of his views on masturbation:

> One must strictly see to it that children rise immediately after awakening in the morning, that they never stay lying awake or

half asleep . . . That is because with this is mostly connected the temptation of thoughts into an unchaste direction. The secret sexual straying of boys as well as girls, well known to doctors, teaches us that we must keep keenly aware of this point already many years before the development of puberty. For this very reason . . . , sleeping in unheated rooms is absolutely to be preferred from now on if this is already not the case. (*Ibid.*, p. 172)

Later he says:

> The child's moral character is exposed to serious dangers emanating from its own body. The widest consequences of these dangers can exercise a devastating effect upon the child's organism. These are the urges connected with sexual development. (p. 256)

He says these "stirrings" can lead a child astray into "surreptitious sins." "Very careful caution is constantly indicated" (p. 256).

The son says "very painful miracles were directed" against his "seminal cord" (*Memoirs*, p. 135). It may be that the son was experiencing as attacks upon his seminal cord the father's expressions of anxiety about masturbation and emissions of semen.

The son did not masturbate. He felt the accusation that he masturbated merited punishment for the accuser; this implies he regarded masturbation as a crime. He says:

> The senior attendant of the Asylum deserves special mention. On the very day of my arrival the voices said that . . . [he had] given false evidence about me in some State enquiry, either on purpose or through carelessness, and particularly to have accused me of masturbation; as punishment for this he had now to be my servant in the form of a fleeting-improvised man. (*Ibid.*, p. 107)

I suppose this is why Schreber has his "accuser" punished. Schreber thinks of masturbating, but condemns the thought as bad, denies the thought is his (though it is), denies the denial, and that anything is denied, denies that the condemnation of the thought is his (though it is), and displaces the condemnation onto a part of himself ("senior attendant") that he splits off from himself, which he imagines thinks, "falsely," that he (Schreber) masturbates. This part of himself sees, rightly, that he (Schreber) thinks of masturbating, but accuses him of masturbating. For the "accuser," as for Schreber who creates him, to think of masturbating is the same as to do it. I infer that Schreber cannot let the accusation stand because he regards the thought of masturbating (or masturbating itself) as so bad. To disaffiliate himself altogether from the "bad" thought of masturbating with which this series of operations began, he condemns the accusation (i.e., the thought of the thought of it) as false and punishes the "accuser." *

Father and son both act as if forbidden by a rule to think directly about the pleasure of masturbation. The father talks about how to avoid children's "temptation" to think of it; he must have thought of masturbation himself: how could someone think of how to help others avoid the "temptation" to think of something without, in some sense, thinking of it himself? His type of thinking, prevalent in the West, is not considered pathological. The son thinks of masturbation and mentions it (though not the pleasure of it), but denies it is he who thinks of it. He disaffiliates himself further from responsibility for the thought by denial of the denial, displacement, splitting, and other operations which together form a complex product which is considered pathological. I regard the labeling of one set of gambits pathological and not the other as simply a convention.

---

* "Fleeting-improvised-men [*flüchtig hingemachte Männer*]," says Schreber, are souls temporarily in human form. They are incomplete, improvised beings, fleetingly improvised, fleeting in their being. He says this state was "some mildly mocking humiliation [which] was to be the lot of those who had sinned in life" (p. 107n). The fleetingness of the senior attendant's punishment could refer to the fleetingness of Schreber's thought of masturbation, and the improvisation of his state to Schreber's improvising him for this episode.

86

The father thinks parents must also "cut off [*abschneiden*]" a child's sexual relations with others.

> When the time draws near for the boy's approach to manhood it is the unavoidable duty of the parents or guardians to cut off the many dangers of chance or casual acquaintanceship with sexual relationships. . . . Experience proves that by far the largest number of those who have succumbed to *lust* in one way or another, have sunk to this state by dint of their original ignorance of the dangers. . . . Such explanatory advice needs to be both more detailed and more weighty when it concerns boys than where girls are involved. (1858, p. 251)

He advises appealing to the boy's "*sense of honour*." What and whose "experience" does he refer to as "proof" of "dangers"? He seems to mean that he fears moral damage ("succumbed to lust") while posing as a doctor, i.e., an expert in applied science.

The son, in explaining feelings of "soul-voluptuousness" he experiences years later, shows the effect of his upbringing upon his thinking:

> Mere low sensuousness can . . . not be considered a motive in my case; were satisfaction of my manly *pride* still possible, I would naturally much prefer it; nor would I ever betray any *sexual lust* in contact with other people. (*Memoirs*, p. 208)

Schreber's father induced children to fear sexual dreams, forbade them (by hints) to masturbate, and deterred their sexual feelings toward others. He was effective with his son:

> Few people have been brought up according to such strict moral principles as I, and have throughout life practised such moderation especially in matters of sex, as I venture to claim for myself. (*Ibid.*, p. 208)

The father's views about sex appear as *negative* images in his son's experiences. The father never endorses or even mentions sexual genital pleasure; nor does the son, except to deny he experienced it. Since the son wrote in detail about feelings in his body, what he fails to say is telling.

87

We know that the son married at thirty-six and did not divorce; we do not know what his sexual life was like when he was not thought mad. His only relationship even resembling a sexual one during his "nervous illness" is with God's "rays" or "nerves" (or with himself). He says he can feel "certain string or cord-like structures" under his skin, all over his body, and especially in his bosom (p. 205). He thinks they attract God's "nerves" or "rays." He believes that when God's "nerves" or "rays" withdraw from him, these structures

> recede by miracle; the effect is that the structures which I call "nerves of voluptuousness" are pushed a little under the surface, that is to say are not so distinctly palpable on the skin, my bosom becomes a little flatter, etc. But when after a short time the rays have to approach again, the "nerves of voluptuousness" . . . become more marked, my bosom bulges again, etc. Such changes occur at present in as short a period as a few minutes. (p. 206)

He writes:

> I can provoke the actual sensation of voluptuousness at any moment by gentle pressure on these structures. I may be excused therefore for retaining the term nerves of voluptuousness. (p. 207)

He says he presses upon these "nerves" "*not for sensual lust*," but because he is

> absolutely compelled to do so if I want to achieve sleep or protect myself against otherwise almost unbearable pain. (p. 205)

This may be all the "sex" the son felt allowed to have, given the calculus of explicit and implicit prohibitions with which he had been raised.

Strange sexual experiences and behavior can arise from restraints placed upon spontaneous sexual pleasure earlier in life. The more odd someone's sexual patterns, the more prohibitions are likely to have been placed upon his or her other, less odd, forms of sexuality. A person's unusual means of sexual (or quasi-sexual) fulfillment may be the only means he feels permitted to use.

Schreber feels aroused in God's presence; he calls this state "soul-voluptuousness." His father had closed or hindered most familiar channels of sexual expression in persons he controlled. I infer that "soul-voluptuousness" is one of few paths the son thinks is open to his sexual energy.

Both Bleuler and Freud discussed the sexuality of people seen as paranoid. Bleuler (1924) said

> It is probably not an accident that in all closely observed paranoiacs . . . I have found a particularly *weak sexuality* which may point to an insufficiency of the impulses generally. . . . (p. 531; italics in original)

Freud understood what he called the megalomania of Schreber, the son, and persons like him on the basis of a withdrawal of "libido," i.e., erotic interest, from people in the environment and from the external world generally (*Standard Edition*, *12*, p. 70 and *14*, p. 74). Neither Bleuler nor Freud considered that "weak sexuality" or a "withdrawal of libido" might be a response to an upbringing that had made it hard to be or do otherwise.

We owe it to Wilhelm Reich, spurned by his professional colleagues, to have underlined the connections between sexual suppression and the type of family he called authoritarian. Sexual needs by their very nature compel contacts with people other than oneself, usually outside one's family of origin. Certain parents, by suppressing sexual acts and feelings in their offspring, *encapsulate* them within the family. Sociologists, East and West, Marxist and capitalist, have neglected to study this sort of family and the possible relation between its prevalence in a society and that society's form of government. Reich was sure the "authoritarian" family is the matrix of the totalitarian state. Curiously, no one has sought to find out if he was right.

Dr. Schreber, by hindering the free development of his son's sexuality, made it hard for the son to give up his ties to his family

89

of origin and to substitute others instead. He impeded his son's genital relations with his own body and with other people. The son, after his second stay in hospital, went to live with his mother; he was then sixty (Baumeyer, 1956, p. 65). And, more significantly, he reveals in his "nervous illness," in his relations with God, that he is still embedded in the *form* of relatedness he had had to his father as a child.

THE LANGUAGE OF THE BODY

The discourse of the unconscious is structured like a language.
The unconscious is the discourse of the Other.

Jacques Lacan

Man's next revolution in his view of himself may come from achievements in the science of linguistics. Possibly, the revolution has already begun.

Recently, a few people have tried to see what can be gained by regarding certain individuals' strange behavior and experiences that hitherto have belonged to the province of psychiatry as evidence, not of illness, but of an unusual way of speaking to others *and* to themselves. Jacques Lacan, a French psychoanalyst, has reexamined Freud's original case histories from this perspective. He has said that "the symptom itself is structured like a language" (Wilden, 1968, p. 32); he believes language supplies the grammar governing what Freud called the unconscious. Lacan considers language the Order, the Law, which society enlists parents to impose upon each infant recruit.

In America, Thomas Szasz (1961), a psychiatrist and psychoanalyst, has likened "so-called mental illnesses" to languages:

91

Although the concept of psychiatry as an analysis of communication is not novel, the full implication of the idea that so-
called mental illnesses may be like languages, and not at all like
diseases of the body, has not been made sufficiently explicit. . . .
We are accustomed to believe that diseases have "causes," "treatments," and "cures." If, however, a person speaks a language
other than our own, we do not usually look for the "cause" of
his peculiar linguistic behavior. It would be foolish—and, of
course, fruitless—to concern ourselves with the "etiology" of
speaking French. To understand such behavior, we must think in
terms of *learning* and *meaning* . . .

If a so-called psychopathological phenomenon is more akin
to a language problem than to illness, it follows that we cannot
meaningfully talk of "treatment" and "cure." Although it is
obvious that under certain circumstances it may be desirable for
a person to change from one language to another—for example
to discontinue speaking French and begin speaking English—this
change is not usually formulated in terms of "treatment." Speaking about learning rather than about etiology permits one to
acknowledge that among a diversity of communicative forms
each has its own *raison d'être*. . . . (pp. 11–12)

Some people believe that what is now called mental illness may
eventually belong to the domain, not of physicians, but of
linguists and communications analysts. In this chapter I attempt
to connect certain experiences considered as signs and symptoms
of mental illness with language patterns. I am not the first person to try to do this but my approach here departs in some
ways from previous ones. I move back and forth between data
and inferences I draw from them. I also suggest a few tentative
steps toward a theory of how language may be linked with
what have been called somatic delusions.

Some of Schreber's odd experiences can be seen as transforms
of speech patterns of his father. The father's wording is figured
upon the ground of the nineteenth-century German language
system. Certain discourse of the father, occurring within that
background, has a style peculiar to him; he often picks unusual

phrases in talking of a child's religious training and relation to God (and to "rays"). I view his choice of idiom as neither accidental, nor meaningless, *nor* without effect upon his son. Parallels exist between certain words he used and events in the son's body which the son construed as his direct experience of God (and "rays").

The father thought children must be intimate with God:

> By frequently repeated gentle reminders the child should be brought to accustom himself to stepping before God at the end of every day alone and in his own mind . . . in order to reflect his *inner self* in the *pure rays* of the concept of God (of the loving Universal *Father*) and to be rewarded by refined will-power. A similar quiet, joyfully thankful look towards heaven should consecrate the morning. (1858, p. 249)

The son during his "holy time" and afterward experiences souls, God, and God's "rays" by means of what he calls "seeing with the mind's eye" (*Memoirs*, p. 47). His experience mirrors his father's words:

> We are used to thinking all impressions we receive from the outer world are mediated through the five senses, particularly that all light and sound sensations are mediated through eye and ear. This may be correct in normal circumstances. However, in the case of a human being who like myself has entered into contact with *rays* and whose head is in consequence so to speak *illuminated by rays*, this is not all. I receive light and sound sensations which are projected direct on to my *inner nervous system* by the *rays;* for their reception the external organs of seeing and hearing are not necessary. (*Ibid.*, p. 117*n*)

Note the similarities:

Father's aim is that the child "reflect his inner self" in the "pure rays of the concept of God."

Son's "inner nervous system" is "illuminated" by God's "rays."

Again, the father calls God, Father.

The father, like so many parents, condemned children's earth-bound sexual feelings; he wished children to become *penetrated* by and to *wed* God:

> The word of religion must not be left simply adhering to ear and mouth, but its deep sense, the spirit of the word, should penetrate and wed the person's soul. The outer revelation and the inner (reason in its highest forms of development) are the two *rays* [*Strahlen*] which the closer they come together the more they are purified of everything human that had been clinging to them until finally they come together at a single point, the point of complete fusion. (1858, p. 254)

The son writes:

> I have frequently referred in this book to the close relationship which exists between voluptuousness and everlasting Blessedness. . . . In order not to be misunderstood, I must point out when I speak of my duty to cultivate voluptuousness, I *never mean any sexual desires towards other human beings (females) least of all sexual intercourse*, but that I have to imagine myself as man and woman in one person having intercourse with myself, or somehow have to achieve with myself a certain sexual excitement etc.—which perhaps under other circumstances might be considered immoral—but which has nothing whatsoever to do with any idea of masturbation or anything like it. (*Memoirs*, p. 208; italics in original)

Here the son explicitly connects masturbation with immorality. His remarkable quasi-sexual experience here can be seen to be a function of his father's deterrence of other sexual relations.

Notice again the likeness between the father's goal and the son's experience:

Father's goal: A "complete fusion" of "two *rays*," "purified of everything human."

94

Son's experience: Imagines he has intercourse as two persons with himself and says he "never"
means "any sexual desires towards other
human beings."

The father says he wants "true religion" to "penetrate" and
"fill" children (1858, p. 241). The son speaks of "divine *rays*"
and God's "nerves" "entering" his body (*Memoirs*, pp. 150, 207,
209, etc.) and of his body being "filled" with "nerves of voluptuousness through the continuous influx of *rays* or God's
nerves" (*ibid.*, p. 207). Father and son use the same word,
Strahlen, translated here as rays. A motto from the title page of
a book of Dr. Schreber (1861b) begins:

> Consider, God lives in your body . . .

The father talks repeatedly of penetrating a child; in a
seventy-five-page stretch of one book (1858) he explicitly recommends penetrating (*dringen* or *eindringen*) a child ten times.

The father's words, I think, signified attitudes toward his son
that he may have displayed by means other than words too.
For example: he treated "pollutions" by enema, thus linking in
the child's mind sexual pleasure with being penetrated.

A child in the penetrated position is in a part usually played
in adult sexual life by a woman. Note the effect of "rays" upon
the son:

> Rays . . . have the power of producing the miracle of unman-
> ning [*Entmannung*]. (*Memoirs*, p. 74)

The son further says:

> In consequence of the miracles directed against me, I had a
> thing between my legs which hardly resembled at all a normally
> formed male organ. (*Ibid.*, p. 77n)

Schreber's hospital records say he maintained he was "a young
girl frightened of indecent assaults" (Baumeyer, 1956, p. 62).

The son often writes of having been or being "unmanned."

95

He felt "unmanning" as an "intended insult" (*Memoirs*, p. 119) and a "threatening ignominy" (*ibid.*, p. 120). "Unmanning" consisted partly in "the (external) male genitals (scrotum and penis) being retracted into the body . . ." (p. 73). The father may have "unmanned" his son, in a sense, long before the son real-ized it.*

In this next passage the father sounds almost as if he is talking about exciting a woman sexually; he says he is discussing educating children:

> The soil of the field to be *cultivated* must be raised, receptive, penetrable, full of sap and strength for a grain of seed [*Samenkorn*] to implant and to rise up. (1860, p. 33)

Samenkorn has sexual associations since *Samen* means semen, sperm.

In relation to God the son adopts a woman's role, not because he wishes to but because he must. It is his "duty," he says, to "*cultivate* feminine feelings" (*Memoirs*, pp. 207–208).

> God demands constant enjoyment. . . . It is my duty to pro-

---

* It is possible to understand the "retraction" of the son's genitals differently, also in terms of his father's behavior. The father put many illustrations into his books of the human figure in a large variety of positions and physical exercises. Niederland (1959a) has pointed out that most of the figures are male and lack genitals, and that a few drawings, in sections dealing with human urinary function, show the genitals, but only as dissected, separate parts of human anatomy. Ritter (1936, p. 11) says the father himself modeled for all the illustrations in his *Pangymnastikon* (1862). The son's negative hallucination, i.e., that he had lost or was losing his genitals, can be linked to his (possible) view of his father's view of his father's body. We could speak here of his identifying with his father.

It may be relevant that the son, like most people in the West who regard God as male, never mentions God's penis.

A syndrome called *koro* (Yap, 1965) occurs in Chinese men in South China and other areas of Southeast Asia; they believe, falsely, that their penises are shrinking into their abdomens. I know of no one who has tried to link *koro* with the upbringing, language patterns, or social life of men in this culture.

vide Him with it in the form of highly developed soul-voluptuousness. . . . (*Ibid.*, p. 209)

A "close relationship" exists "between voluptuousness and everlasting Blessedness" (p. 208):

> This state of Blessedness is mainly a state of voluptuous enjoyment, which for its full development needs the fantasy of either being or wishing to be a female being, which naturally is not to my taste. (p. 240)

I regard the son's "cultivation" of "feminine feelings" in relation to God as an *image*, as an adult version, a disguised expression, of events his father's words could have stimulated in his body years before.

A child in the father's view is like God's woman in another respect; he receives "seeds" from God which grow inside him.

> At a tender age the ground must be made ready *to receive the seed* [*Samenkorn*] *of Godliness.* (1858, p. 134)

> The presentiment of Godliness, the slight God consciousness, is the most noble *seed* [*Keim*] of the human spirit. . . . (*Ibid.*, p. 154)

> It is the parent's task to tend [the child's] noble seeds [*Keime*] properly. . . . These seeds [*Keime*] are man's *dowry.* (p. 23)

Keim (plural *Keime*) has sexual connotations. It is a masculine noun meaning seed, germ, bud. *Keim* as a feminine noun means gonad and *Keimzelle* means germ-cell.

The metaphor of the dowry, which the father uses often, makes the child God's bride. Had the father lived, he might have been astonished (and dismayed) to see how well indeed he had "made ready" the "ground" for the "seed of Godliness" in his son's body. His son says he felt within himself a

> quickening like the first signs of life of a human embryo: by a divine miracle *God's nerves* corresponding to *male seed* had been thrown into my body. (*Memoirs*, p. 43n)

97

The son says a "consequence of unmanning" is *"fertilization* by divine rays" (*ibid.,* p. 148). The father calls education "the second procreation" (1860, p. 10).

Dr. Schreber *instructed* (by implication) the son to perform the operation of "assimilating" words into bodily experience.

> Even in the most highly cultured human languages a word that serves to designate purely spiritual conditions, feelings, or abstract, immaterial, or figurative concepts only attains the concept it is supposed to be expressing in an approximative way, never completely; the word cannot communicate the concept in a fully *embodied* [*verkörpert*] form from one man to another; rather, the other man's own independent activity is required in order to make the concept comprehensible to his individual understanding in order to extract the concept from the word. . . . Every higher concept is to its word as the spirit to the body. . . . Just as a foodstuff introduced into the body cannot nourish it directly but rather does so as the substance undergoes the processes of digestion, blood formation, etc., and in this manner gets assimilated, so it is also with the word, especially those which designate abstract concepts. (1858, p. 253. Dr. Schreber italicizes this whole passage.)

There is evidence that the son did "embody" his father's words, though not in ways the father had foreseen.

I wonder how often, and how, certain parents teach children to embody words, and if parents of offspring with somatic complaints do it especially effectively.

Speakers of Indo-European languages, such as English or nineteenth-century German, in order to express events occurring in and between minds, often use words and idioms that literally denote events in and between bodies (Whorf, 1964). In English, I may feel touched, touchy, or in or out of touch with myself or you; I may feel hearty or heartbroken, have or lack guts or backbone; someone may chew my ear off, get under my skin, turn my stomach, swell my head, etc. I surmise that these terms refer to and reflect events occurring almost simultaneously, usually outside awareness, in the bodies of those who use them. If I speak of touching *you*, breaking *your* heart, getting under *your* skin, etc., I can create events in your body.

Certain heard words, especially if heard often and in childhood, may be encoded or transformed, stored, and, later, in disguise, retrieved and reexperienced. I think everyone, some of the time, and some people, nearly all the time, recurrently experience in and with their bodies literal meanings of certain oft-repeated phrases they heard in childhood. That is, they retranslate words back into the same modality of bodily experience from which those who spoke the words derived them from within their own bodies. We could call it *imaging* to transpose spoken words into other modalities of experience and to experience words so transposed.

Some, possibly all, people's bodies resonate to others' spoken words, inscribe transforms of the words, store them, and later reexperience them. Certain persons who do this sort of thing often and well seem unaware they are doing it. I think people called hypochondriacs are either talented at it (and unaware they are), or have heard more "physicalistic" speech in childhood than most people, or both. Schreber's doctors regarded him as a hypochondriac.

Perhaps the prevalence of certain bodily complaints in a culture is connected with idioms it uses. For instance, backaches and back pains are endemic to the United States and England. Americans and Englishmen speak of having someone on their backs, being stabbed in the back, being or having a pain in the neck or arse, lacking backbone or backing, getting someone's back up, backbreaking work, backbiting, backfiring, backlash, etc. Americans and Englishmen express a large number of interpersonal irritations in language that may, I suggest, both mirror and bring on feelings in their backs. Possibly some day we shall speak of *lingua*somatic or psycho*semantic*, not psychosomatic, illnesses.

It is easy in principle to prove or disprove that parents, by language, can induce odd bodily events years later in offspring. Listen to parents talk. See what guesses, if any, can be made about strange bodily experiences in their offspring. Ask the offspring some years later about their experiences. Compare guesses with data. My impression, based on knowing well many families (including my own), is that certain investigators could score a high percentage of correct guesses with certain families. Such a study has not been done. Therefore I must regard the theory I present here as provisional.

I have generally confined myself in this book to inferences about Schreber's father's behavior toward his children. Only occasionally have I attributed experiences to him. I have not used these attributions as primary data; nor do I here. However, I should like to note that the father in his language behavior implies that he may have wished to penetrate children. Possibly, he experienced his sons, at least partly, as women and somehow conveyed this to them. It would be interesting to know what *his* sexual life was like.

The father, while appearing to *order* children, may be *reporting* at the same time events in his body without meaning to do so. Possibly the author of the *Memoirs* understood this and, in ascribing to God certain wishes and motives toward him, was remembering wishes and motives he once had ascribed to his father.

Schreber's father, speaking about relations between adolescents and parents, writes:

> Once the childlike mind is completely *penetrated* by love and respect and all the *warm rays* which *gush forth* from them, the will of the child is ruled more and more from this perspective and is led gently towards the pure and noble direction. (1858, p. 235)

The context of this passage makes clear that it is parents who must "completely" "penetrate," in some sense, children—boys and girls—with "warm rays" which "gush." An adolescent boy, hearing these terms from his father, might guess they refer to and reflect events the father was experiencing in his penis whether or not the boy was guessing it "consciously." The boy also might experience corresponding, *reciprocal* events in *his* body, especially if he had been told to convert words into body experience.

Clinical folklore about people considered schizophrenic holds that they are more aware of other persons' "unconscious" minds than most people are. Perhaps they are more attuned and responsive to messages that anyone in the same position would receive, but that few people would be affected by or even notice.

If Schreber's father were transmitting sexual messages to his children, he was doing so covertly, not explicitly. And, I assume, he would have denied it to all others and probably to himself. It seems probable, given the official, repressive attitudes toward sex of the Schreber family and their society, that the father *and* his children would have kept secret from themselves and each other both his emission of sexual messages and their reception of them.

If a father's feelings toward a son are implied only, and never openly acknowledged, the son could find it hard to connect them with any effect they might have upon him.

A child's view of his parents' feelings toward him (whether or not their feelings are explicit) generally is or becomes a critical dimension of the child's view of himself. A parent's view of oneself in early childhood can affect how one sees oneself for the rest of one's life. One can refuse to hold a position a parent assigns oneself, although refusal may not be easy, but one cannot not deal with the parent's placing oneself there, especially if the parent does it often. If a boy sees his father regarding him as someone to be penetrated, cultivated, or implanted with seeds, it could become his form of personal relatedness to wish to feel, or to feel and wish *not* to feel, penetrated, cultivated, or implanted with seeds.

Here is an outline of my set of inferences:

Father's experience of his body   Son's experience of his body
in relation to his son   (probably forgotten and only
                         years later remembered)

Father's words to son _ _ _ _ → Son's perception of father's
                                 words

What Edwin Sapir, the American linguist, said could apply to this situation: "The word, as we know, is not only a key, it may also be a fetter." It is as if the sounds of the father's words, trapping and trapped in the son's body, speak silently. They appear transformed as words again in the son's report of his body experiences. The son's body was speaking, but no one was listening.

To free himself from his bizarre relation to God, the son may have needed to see certain of his bodily feelings as *transforms* of his father's words and to see that he was obeying his father's wishes to so transform them.* (To hear [*hören*] or to hearken [*horchen*] has the same root in German as to obey [*gehorchen*].) He would not have needed to recall from mem-

---

* In the yogic tradition a *mantra*, i.e., a mystical sound formula, is supposed to give rise to a distinct vibration by which the one who utters it can make the thing or deity that resonates to that frequency appear.

> According to the Mantrayāna ("Path of the Mantra") School, there is associated with each object and element of nature and with each organic creature, sub-human, human, and super-human, including the highest orders of deities . . . a particular rate of vibration. If this be known and formulated as sound in a *Mantra* and used expertly by a perfected *Yogi*, . . . it is held to be capable . . . in the case of spiritual beings, of impelling the lesser deities to emit telepathically their divine influence in *rays of grace*. (Evans-Wentz, 1969, p. 37*n*)

One usually uses the mantric sound to make manifest a deity and his rays of grace to oneself. Dr. Schreber's sounds have made God, I think, appear to his son. I know of no word in the mantric or any other tradition for that maneuver.

ory which words; they were in books all over Germany. Neither he, nor his doctors, nor anyone else thought to look there.

We use several known channels to report events in our own bodies and, I believe, to create events in others' bodies. People "speak," for instance, not only with words, but by the rate, pitch, and volume of their speech, by paralinguistic sounds (grunts, coughs, breath sounds, etc.), and by body posture and movements. We may also employ unknown, *chemical* channels: Harry Wiener (1966), an American physician, discusses the probability that we emit and receive messages by "external chemical messengers" (his term) contained in sweat, urine, saliva, tears, breath, and other body discharges. We use words to support, deny, and conceal messages we convey, often simultaneously, by other channels.

Ray Birdwhistell (1970), an American anthropologist, says if two human beings were put in an elaborate box to record all the informational signal units—"minimally discernible changes in the sound, light, and odour stream"—they emitted and could potentially receive,

> probably the lifetime efforts of roughly half the adult population in the United States would be required to sort the units deposited on one tape record in the course of an hour's interaction between the two subjects! (pp. 3–4)

Of course, we can never retrieve this sort of information from Schreber's family of origin. I am pointing to routes along which the study of the *language* of insanity and sanity has already begun.

In many first-person reports of religious experiences, the subject virtually seems to be describing a sexual experience; the "sexual" partner is present in the spirit, not the flesh. The Catholic Church has made saints of some such subjects, partly owing to their spiritual (or quasi-sexual) experiences.

Should *all* religious experiences, quasi-sexual or not, be regarded *only* as transforms of interpersonal events in the subjects' childhoods? Is this all that "revelations" reveal? Jung thought that religious experience is not traceable to post-natal events, but is part of our transindividual heritage. (He was familiar with Schreber's *Memoirs* and says [1962, p. 300*n*] he drew Freud's attention to it; he does not mention the father's writings.) Certain investigators have begun to classify the varieties of religious experience. Which varieties are based on repressed childhood memories? If any are not, where (or Who) is their source?

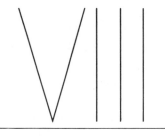

FREUD'S ANALYSIS

It remains for the future to decide whether there is more
delusion in my theory than I should like to admit, or
whether there is more truth in Schreber's delusion than
other people are as yet prepared to believe.

Any one who was more daring than I am in making inter-
pretations, or who was in touch with Schreber's family
and consequently better acquainted with the society in
which he moved and the small events of his life, would
find it an easy matter to trace back innumerable details
of his delusions to their sources and so discover their
meaning . . .

Sigmund Freud

Freud provided a thorough theory of *Homo psychologicus.*
But in order to understand how persons affect each other we
need to modify the system of ideas he and his followers have
furnished us.

Psychoanalysts say their patients (and all people) relate to
objects, internal and external. By objects they nearly always
mean persons or parts of persons—not things—who are the objects of their patients' (and other people's) acts or feelings.

When psychoanalysts call a person an object, it is a person of a kind who is not and could not be alive. For instance, the object, in psychoanalytic theory, never acts or experiences; it cannot affect or be affected by anyone; it cannot see, feel, know, plan, wish, hope, or act. Psychoanalysts use the term to represent a person, but the person it represents is not real.

The unfolding of an individual occurs in the context of, and can be defined by, the development of his relations with others. Real other people are *agents* like ourselves. If I am to understand someone, I must assume he has lived among people who engage in the same form of activity I attribute to him. Of course, psychoanalysts know that other persons act upon their patients and that certain persons who dealt with their patients as children influenced them greatly by their behavior. But insofar as they speak of object-relations, their theory does not adequately account for this influence.

Theories of object-relations in their present form developed long after Freud's analysis in 1911 of Daniel Paul Schreber. But parts of Freud's analysis of Schreber can be seen as precursors of these theories.

Freud chose as data certain of Schreber's conscious experiences. To explain his data—Schreber's conscious experiences—he ascribed to Schreber's mind events of which he assumed Schreber was unaware. Freud disregarded as data the father's writings.

He saw Schreber as paranoid. In his paper on Schreber he said:

> What lies at the core of the conflict in cases of paranoia among males is a homosexual wishful phantasy of *loving a man* . . . (*Standard Edition, 12*, p. 62)

Freud thought the paranoid man contradicts his love for a man by hating the man:

> "I do not *love* him—I *hate* him." This contradiction, which must have run thus in the unconscious, cannot, however, become

conscious to a paranoic in this form. The mechanism of symptom-formation in paranoia requires that internal perceptions—feelings—shall be replaced by external perceptions. Consequently the proposition "I hate him" becomes transformed by *projection* into another one "*He hates* (persecutes) *me*, which will justify me in hating him." And thus the impelling unconscious feeling makes its appearance as though it were the consequence of an external perception:

"I do not *love* him—I *hate* him, because HE PERSECUTES ME." (*Ibid.*, pp. 62–63; italics in the original)

To paraphrase Freud, if a man loves a man and feels he is forbidden to, he denies his love and changes it to its opposite; "I love him" becomes "I hate him" by denial and reversal. If he feels unjustified in hating him he changes his hatred to its inverse: "I hate him" becomes "He hates me" by projection. This type of projection, though not all types, can be regarded as a reversal in syntax: the subject and object of the sentence "I hate him" exchange places.

A man who thinks he is persecuted gets to that position by making three operations upon his homosexual love: denial, reversal, and projection. These steps keep him unaware of "bad" feelings. He is unconscious of loving a man, of the steps he takes to keep himself unconscious, and, I presume, of his motives for keeping the love unconscious and for keeping unconscious the steps to keep it unconscious.

I believe a mind can use the same sequence of operations— denial, reversal, and projection*—in relation to any desires it forbids itself.

---

* Recently, some fascinating research has given support to large parts of Freud's theory of the mind. Herman A. Witkin and Helen B. Lewis (1967), American psychologists, have studied in a sleep and dream laboratory the ways in which the mind transforms (their word) known presleep experiences, such as watching films, into dreams. Their findings are compatible with Freud's views about the types of operations the mind performs in its "dream work." These operations resemble the sorts of transformations Freud suggests everyone applies to certain childhood experiences.

The father, in Freud's analysis of Schreber, is not an agent. He is for Freud an object toward which the son's desire is directed. But he (or it) in no way governs, determines, limits, opposes, suppresses, fears, desires, rouses, inflames, sustains, acknowledges, or even knows of his son's alleged desire for him; the same is so for any desire his son could ever have. Although Freud's theory of why Schreber felt persecuted is consistent with my view that Schreber's father may have secretly stirred up Schreber sexually, his theory does not deal with the father's probable behavior.

Every relationship between a parent and child is unique. In order to understand a given relationship, it is best to start with a minimum of presuppositions and to obtain as many facts as possible. If one aims to ascertain a given sector of that relationship, such as the child's feelings toward the parent, it would be helpful to have an idea of how *this* parent experiences and treats the child. To understand Schreber's feelings toward his flesh-and-blood father or toward his internalized father, it is pertinent to know what feelings in particular his father's behavior would have been likely to elicit in him.

Schreber's father, in fact, went on at length teaching parents how to persuade, instruct, cajole, and beguile their children to love them starting "at the earliest age . . . long before the development of language" (1858, pp. 131–134). More relevantly,

---

Stanislav Grof (1970), a Czechoslovakian psychiatrist now working in the United States, has treated more than fifty persons, representing "all major psychiatric diagnostic categories," with serial LSD sessions, fifteen to eighty sessions a person, combined with drug-free psychotherapy. He found that experiences from the early sessions (though not the later) "could be understood by and large within the Freudian framework. . . . Many of the experiences from this stage could almost be considered a 'laboratory' proof of the basic Freudian concepts" (p. 61). Grof found the writings of Otto Rank (1952), Carl Jung, and scholars of mystical experience more applicable than Freud's to the later phases of the therapy.

Neither Witkin and Lewis nor Grof mention Freud's theory of paranoia in these studies.

he may, as we saw in the last chapter, have also, probably unwittingly, excited his sons sexually.

Given what can reasonably be inferred about how the father
treated his sons in other respects, it is likely that they would
have *hated* him if they could have (and would have felt justified in hating him). The father taught parents to stop children
from feeling "spite," "anger," and "bitterness" toward their
parents; these feelings can be classed as *hatred*. Therefore, his
sons may have needed to be concerned with how not to hate
their father. Karl Menninger (1942), referring to Freud's analysis of Schreber, wrote:

> The man who feels himself persecuted is obviously defending
> himself not against his love of someone so much as against his
> hate for someone, someone whom the persecutor represents. He
> defends himself by saying, "It is not I who hate him, but he
> who hates me." (p. 262*n*)

His conclusion, reached by reasoning unlike mine, is compatible
with my findings.

Of course, in Freud's view, to hate or love someone means to
hate *and* love him. Did Schreber fear his love for his father? Perhaps; however, I see no need to assume it to explain his feelings
of persecution, since they can be adequately explained as *transforms* of his *real* persecution.

Freud had already believed that paranoia arises as a "defence"
against homosexual love before studying the Schreber case. He
said:

> I can . . . call a friend and fellow-specialist to witness that I
> had developed my theory of paranoia before I became acquainted
> with the contents of Schreber's book. (*Standard Edition, 12,*
> p. 79)

He selected as his data passages from the *Memoirs* he thought
strengthened his thesis. Every scientist *takes* as his data a part,
generally a tiny fragment, from the given; what are usually
called data, i.e., the given, could perhaps be called *capta*, i.e., the

taken. It is rare, especially in psychology and the social sciences, for anyone to study anything without choosing from the given mainly material which supports views one already holds. Freud does not deal with Schreber's "miracles," although Schreber said they were his major source of suffering. It is to Freud's credit that in his introduction to his discussion of Schreber he asked his readers to read Schreber's *Memoirs* at least once before going on to his own analysis (*ibid.*, p. 11).

Some of Freud's data accord with his theory only if one presupposes both his constructions upon his data and his theory to be true. The same data could be construed differently and could sustain other theories. Consider for instance this passage from Freud:

> . . . I shall consider myself justified in maintaining the view that *the basis of Schreber's illness was the outburst of a homosexual impulse.* This hypothesis harmonises with a noteworthy detail of the case history, which *remains otherwise inexplicable.* The patient had a fresh "nervous collapse," which exercised a decisive effect upon the course of his illness, at a time when his wife was taking a short holiday on account of her own health. Up till then she had spent several hours with him every day and had taken her mid-day meal with him. But when she returned after an absence of four days, she found him most sadly altered: so much so, indeed, that he himself no longer wished to see her. "What especially determined my mental breakdown was a particular night, during which I had quite an extraordinary number of emissions—quite half a dozen, all in that one night" [*Memoirs,* p. 68]. It is easy to understand that the mere presence of his wife must have acted as a *protection against the attractive power of the men about him;* and if we are prepared to admit that an emission cannot occur in an adult without some mental concomitant, we shall be able to supplement the patient's emissions that night by assuming that they were *accompanied by homosexual phantasies which remained unconscious.* (p. 45)

This set of events "harmonises" with Freud's "hypothesis" that "the basis of Schreber's illness was the outburst of a homosexual impulse" only if one assumes that (a) Schreber's emissions "were accompanied by homosexual phantasies" and (b) the "presence of his wife must have acted as a protection" against his homosexual wishes. Both assumptions depend upon Freud's *hypothesis* that Schreber had homosexual desires. Freud, in this section of his essay, is first trying to establish Schreber's homosexuality and offers these data as supporting evidence. But these data draw force as testimony to uphold Freud's premise from the premise which Freud supposes they uphold. His interpretation of this episode is part of his proof for the theory upon which the interpretation rests. This particular logical weakness in Freud's use of data is not uncommon in his writings. It is a form of what logicians call *petitio principii:* the fallacy of taking for granted in a line of argument a premise which depends upon the conclusion.

This passage from the *Memoirs* does *not* "remain otherwise inexplicable" if one uses Schreber's father's writings as data. For instance, I have already connected the occurrence of Schreber's "nervous collapse," after a night of many emissions, with his father's anti-"pollutions" campaign. Possibly, Schreber's wife's presence had been protecting him until now from the influence of his father's decrees against sex. Perhaps in her absence he recalled his father's fears of "pollutions" *and* his father's edicts against other forms of sex too. And maybe this is why he no longer wished to see her.

Freud acknowledges he knows nothing of Schreber's childhood. Yet he says of Schreber:

> His father's most dreaded threat, castration, actually provided the material for his wish-phantasy (at first resisted but later accepted) of being transformed into a woman. (p. 56)

Where is Freud's evidence? Freud comes to think this about Schreber, I presume, because he holds the dread of castration to be virtually universal.

From where does the dread come? Does Freud propose that

sons imagine their fathers threaten them with castration, even if the fathers do not? If so, then sons, in Freud's view, are *paranoid*. Does he suppose fathers do threaten sons with castration? Literally or metaphorically? Only sons or daughters too? All fathers or only some? If they do, why do they? And if they do, literally or metaphorically, they are *persecuting* their offspring. If so, why does Freud ignore this in his theory of paranoia? Remember: Schreber assumed he had been "unmanned." If Freud reckoned that Schreber's father had threatened him with castration, might it not have behooved him to look for hints of it in the father's writings? Or did he conceive that Schreber would "naturally" have feared castration no matter what his father thought or did?

We shall deal with these issues by situating them in the context of (1) certain views Freud held about the development of the mind, (2) the beliefs of nineteenth-century physicians and parents about masturbation and methods of *treatment* they used for it, and (3) Freud's case study of "Little Hans."

(1)

—

Freud presumed all boys and men fear castration, however repressed their fear. He called the fear the castration complex. He linked it with a cluster of feelings he named the Oedipus complex. He thought:

> the Oedipus complex may justly be regarded as the nucleus of the neuroses. (*Standard Edition, 16*, p. 337)

In his view, it is also the "nuclear complex" for nonneurotic people. He supposed that fathers, in both the castration and Oedipus complexes, play the part of a "dreaded enemy" who threatens castration.

Everyone, avers Freud, is fated from *before birth* to endure and deal with an Oedipus complex in childhood: everyone loves one's parent of the opposite sex and fears and hates one's parent of the same sex. Everyone also undergoes, usually less intensely, an "inverted" Oedipus complex: one loves the parent of the same sex and fears and hates the parent of the opposite sex. Freud suggests that this state prevails in children who later become homosexual. He believes it leads a boy or man to *wish* to lose his male genitals.

Freud thought his views were confirmed

> by a legend that has come down to us from classical antiquity: . . . . What I have in mind is the legend of King Oedipus and Sophocles' drama which bears his name.

> Oedipus, son of Laius, King of Thebes, and of Jocasta, was exposed as an infant because an oracle had warned Laius that the still unborn child would be his father's murderer. The child was rescued, and grew up as a prince in an alien court, until, in doubts as to his origin, he too questioned the oracle and was warned to avoid his home since he was destined to murder his father and take his mother in marriage. On the road leading away from what he believed was his home, he met King Laius and slew him in a sudden quarrel. He came next to Thebes and solved the riddle set him by the Sphinx who barred his way. Out of gratitude the Thebans made him their king and gave him Jocasta's hand in marriage. He reigned long in peace and honour, and she who, unknown to him, was his mother bore him two sons and two daughters. Then at last a plague broke out and the Thebans made enquiry once more of the oracle. It is at this point that Sophocles' tragedy opens. The messengers bring back the reply that the plague will cease when the murderer of Laius has been driven from the land.

> > But he, where is he? Where shall now be read
> > The fading record of this ancient guilt?

> The action of the play consists in nothing other than the process of revealing, with cunning delays and ever-mounting excitement —a process that can be likened to the work of a psychoanalysis— that Oedipus himself is the murderer of Laius, but further that he is the son of the murdered man and of Jocasta. Appalled at

the abomination which he has unwittingly perpetrated, Oedipus blinds himself and forsakes his home. The oracle has been fulfilled. . . . (*Standard Edition, 4,* pp. 260–262)

Freud thinks Oedipus' blinding, like blinding in fantasies and myths generally, stands for castration.

> If *Oedipus Rex* moves a modern audience no less than it did the contemporary Greek one, the explanation can only be . . . looked for in the particular nature of the material . . . There must be something which makes a voice within us ready to recognise the compelling force of destiny in the *Oedipus.* . . . And a factor of this kind is in fact involved in the story of King Oedipus. His destiny moves us only because it might have been ours—because the oracle laid the same curse upon us before our birth as upon him. It is the fate of all of us, perhaps, to direct our first sexual impulse towards our mother and our first hatred and our first murderous wish against our father. Our dreams convince us that this is so. King Oedipus, who slew his father Laius and married his mother Jocasta, merely shows us the fulfillment of our own childhood wishes. . . . While the poet, as he unravels the past, brings to light the guilt of Oedipus, he is at the same time compelling us to recognise our own inner minds, in which those same impulses, though suppressed, are still to be found. (*Ibid.,* pp. 262–263)

Freud says Oedipus' fate "shows us the fulfillment of our own childhood wishes." What does *Laius'* behavior show us? In certain versions of the myth, including the one Sophocles used, Laius, fearing his newborn son would kill him, snatched him from his nurse's arms, pierced his feet with a nail, bound them together, and left him to die (Graves, 1960, *2,* p. 9). Oedipus means swollen foot.

Laius had previously been an active homosexual. George Devereux (1953), an American anthropologist, says:

> Numerous Greek sources and fragments reveal that Laius was deemed to have been the inventor of pederasty. In his early manhood, long before he married Jocasta and fathered Oedipus,

114

Laius fell violently in love with Chrysippus, son of King Pelops.
. . . He chose to kidnap him. . . . The enraged Pelops . . . laid
upon Laius the curse that his own son should slay him and then
marry his own mother. According to a later version it is . . .
Zeus' decision that Laius' son would kill him in retribution for
the rape of Chrysippus. This curse seems to suggest that the
Greek mind linked Oedipus with Chrysippus—an inference which
is further substantiated by still another version of this myth, according to which Hera was so greatly angered by the rape of
Chrysippus that she sent the Sphinx to ravage Thebes, in order
to punish the Thebans for having tolerated Laius' homosexual
escapade. The *Oidipodeia* is even more specific in conjoining the
fates of Chrysippus and of Oedipus. According to this epic,
Oedipus was exposed as a propitiatory sacrifice, in order to ap-
pease Hera's wrath over the Chrysippus incident. In other words,
Hera caused Laius to lose not only his youthful bedfellow Chrysippus, but also his son Oedipus. (p. 133)

Freud almost certainly knew this part of the myth; Otto Rank,
his close disciple for many years, reported it (1912). Yet Freud
mentions it nowhere in discussing the Oedipus myth or complex.

If a son's feelings of persecution can be understood as a defense against homosexual love, a father's persecution of a son
can be understood by the same rules of inference also as a defense against homosexual love.

Freud's analysis of the Oedipus myth omits Laius' persecution
of Chrysippus and Oedipus. Yet a close copy of Freud's schema
for analyzing Schreber can apply to Laius with equal validity:

> What lies at the core of the conflict in Laius is a homo-
> sexual wishful fantasy of *loving a boy* . . .
>
> Laius contradicts his love for a boy by persecuting a boy
> ("I do not *love* him—I shall *kill* him") and replaces "internal
> perceptions—feelings" by "external perceptions."
>
> Consequently the proposition "I shall kill him" becomes
> transformed by *projection* into another one, "*He will kill*

(persecute) *me*, which will justify me in killing him." And thus the impelling unconscious feeling makes its appearance as though it were the consequence of an external perception:

"I do not *love* him—I shall *kill* him, because HE WISHES TO KILL (PERSECUTE) ME."

As Schreber displaces his "object" from his father at the start of the schema to God at the end, so Laius displaces his "object" from Chrysippus to Oedipus.

Devereux says:

> It is striking to note that psychoanalytic theory pays exceedingly little attention to certain complexes which, in a very genuine sense, complement the Oedipus complex. (1953, p. 132)

He states that psychoanalytic writers generally neglect the sadistic and homosexual components of what he says "may be called the *Laius complex*." He assumes this failure to deal with the "complementary Oedipus complex"

> is rooted in the adult's deep-seated need to place all responsibility for the Oedipus complex upon the child, and to ignore, whenever possible, certain parental attitudes which actually stimulate the infant's oedipal tendencies. This *deliberate* scotoma is probably rooted in the *authoritarian atmosphere characteristic of nineteenth-century family life*. . . . (*Ibid.*, p. 132)

Many of Freud's early patients whom he classified as hysterics (most would now be seen as schizophrenic) told him that adults had seduced them in childhood. At first Freud believed them and considered their hysterical symptoms to be derived from memories of these experiences. Later he came to disbelieve them; and still later he came to think his patients were remembering not real seductions, but their *fantasies* of seduction. He compared these fantasies to the "imaginary creations of paranoics which become conscious as delusions" (*Standard Edition*, 7, p. 275).

Possibly, his patients were remembering their *parents'* sexual fantasies toward them, expressed through turns of phrase (of the sort Dr. Schreber used), glances, facial expressions, and the like.

(2)

The list of physicians who thought masturbation damages minds, brains, or bodies reads like a *Who's Who* of nineteenth-century psychiatry.* I have compiled this catalog (which is only a sample) of the supposed consequences of "self-abuse" from writings of some leading doctors, mainly psychiatrists, of the last century:

Apathy, despair, irritability, surliness, dullness of sentiment, loss of self-respect, obsessions, compulsions, conceit, mischievous disposition, idleness, premature ejaculation, impotence, sexual anesthesia, aversion to coitus, hypochondriasis, agitation, melancholia, hysteria, neurasthenia (i.e., nervous debility), delusions, hallucinations, mania, catatonia, insanity, homicidal tendencies, and suicide;

too much (*and* too little) blood flow to the brain, brain exhaustion, stupor, paralysis, tabes dorsalis, deterioration of vision, epilepsy, vertigo, memory loss, feeble-mindedness, idiocy, imbecility, and dementia;

asthma, dyspepsia (i.e., indigestion), dysuria (i.e., difficult or painful urination), tuberculosis, functional disorders of the heart, cancer, uterine hemorrhage, leukorrhea (i.e., vaginal discharge), falling of the womb, stunted growth,

---

* The remarkable history of the attitudes and activities of medicine and psychiatry toward masturbation in the past two hundred years has been reviewed by R. A. Spitz (1953), E. H. Hare (1962), J. Duffy (1963), A. Comfort (1967), and T. Szasz (1970); see also the articles by Lea, Sturgis, and Sutor in R. E. L. Masters (1967).

debility, emaciation, marasmus (i.e., wasting of the body), and death.

Masturbation was also regarded as the *result* of insanity: anyone who valued his sanity so little as to masturbate could not be sane from the start.

E. H. Hare (1962), an English psychiatrist who traces the rise and fall of the idea that masturbation is an important cause of mental disorder, says:

> There were more subtle dangers. It was believed that every youth who masturbated endangered the vitality of his future children; and for 200 years the horrid phantom of racial decay terrified the physicians and educators of the western world . . . Physicians saw themselves as the guardians of civilisation; they proclaimed it the duty of parents and teachers to prevent by all means the habit of masturbation in the young; and they believed that whereas in adolescence an appeal to reason or the picture of future disease might suffice, in children the most satisfactory method of prevention was the *threat of an immediate and alarming punishment.* (pp. 16–17)

Doctors, teachers, and parents designed, threatened, and practiced treatments to prevent masturbation in suspected or confessed masturbators of all ages, especially children and adolescents. Since doctors thought many mental patients had become or remained ill because of masturbating, they imposed upon them antimasturbation remedies. Methods used against both sexes included:

> Castration, circumcision, locked chastity belts, corporal punishment, faradization (i.e., application of electricity) to the spine, cautery of the spine and genitals, and, before going to sleep, tying the hands or confining them in bags, and, in order to hinder lying on the back, tying bags of pebbles to the back.

Against men and boys:

Enclosing the penis in bandages, infibulation (the placement of metal wires or rings through the prepuce in order to forestall its retraction behind the glans), section of the dorsal nerves of the penis in order to prevent sensations in and erections of the penis, blistering of the prepuce, and wearing spiked or toothed metal rings on the penis at night, which would bite into the penis if it became erect.

Against women and girls:

Ovariotomy (i.e., cutting into an ovary), clitoridectomy (i.e., removal of the clitoris), infibulation of the prepuce and labia majora, surgical separation of the preputial hood from the clitoris, blistering of the prepuce, vulva, and insides of the thighs, and, before going to sleep, putting the legs in splints, or tying them one to either side of the crib or bed.

René Spitz (1953), an American psychoanalyst who extensively surveyed the literature on masturbation, says that

. . . between 1850 and 1879 *surgical treatment* was recommended more frequently than any of the other measures. . . . (p. 120)

A president of the Royal College of Surgeons, James Hutchinson (1891), recommended circumcision for masturbators, and said

that measures *more radical than circumcision* would . . . be a true kindness to many patients of both sexes. (quoted by Hare, 1962, p. 22)

Alex Comfort (1967), an English writer and biologist, says that over the latter part of the nineteenth century

there was a truly remarkable upsurge of what can only be termed comic-book sadism. The advocacy of these bizarre therapies was not confined to eccentrics. By about 1880 the individual who might wish for unconscious reasons to tie, chain, or infibulate sexually active children or mental patients—the two most readily available captive audiences—to adorn them with grotesque appliances, encase them in plaster of paris, leather, or rubber, to beat, frighten, *or even castrate them,* to cauterise or denervate the genitalia, could find humane and respectable medical authority for doing so in good conscience. Masturbational insanity was now real enough—it was affecting the medical profession. (pp. 103–104)

Paul Emil Flechsig (1847–1929), an eminent neuroanatomist and psychiatrist, was Schreber's doctor during the first and the early part of the second occurrences of his "nervous illness" and he was the director of the clinic where Schreber was an inpatient. He *castrated* (1884) at least three inmates of this clinic to put right their nervous and psychological disorders. Flechsig, in reporting his "success" with these cases and reviewing current literature on the value of castration in psychiatry, concludes:

> I . . . think there are justifiable grounds to use castration as a successful treatment against neurosis and psychosis.* (p. 468)

Bloch (1908) says physicians, in order to treat masturbation, appeared before the child armed with great knives and scissors,

---

* Many experiences and acts of patients in mental hospitals seen by staff as symptoms of a disease "process" can also be seen as patients' responses to staff's behavior; for an example of this, see Schatzman, 1970.

I do not think Schreber's relationship with Flechsig and his attendants originally occasioned Schreber's "unmanning," but that relationship could have contributed to it. Schreber often connects Flechsig or Flechsig's "soul" with his "unmanning"; for instance:

> Small parts of Flechsig's soul . . . used repeatedly to exclaim as if astonished "Is he not unmanned yet?" (*Memoirs,* p. 119)

Schreber probably knew Flechsig used castration as treatment. Patients in mental hospitals learn quickly about therapies used there. It is also likely Schreber had read Flechsig's reports about it: patients of a famous doctor often read his writings and Schreber read widely in psychiatry.

Schreber could have been saying: "I already am, or am being, unmanned; therefore, there is no need for Flechsig to unman me."

and threatened a painful operation or even to cut off the genital organs. (quoted by Hare, 1962, p. 23)

Girls were also told their hands would be cut off. Hare writes:

> It is certain that during the latter half of the nineteenth century little boys (and little girls too) commonly suffered the threat of genital amputation, and we may deduce that the *frequency with which Freud's early patients remembered this threat reflected the fashionable belief* of their parents in the importance of preventing masturbation. (*Ibid.*, p. 23)

Given the procedures practiced against masturbators and mental patients, threats of castration were credible.

Struwwelpeter (Shock-headed Peter) was a famous nineteenth-century children's book. Dr. Heinrich Hoffman, a Frankfurt pediatrician, wrote it in German in 1845; it has passed through many editions and translations. Here is an excerpt entitled "The Story of Little Suck-A-Thumb" from the English *Struwwelpeter*.

> One day, Mamma said: "Conrad dear.
> I must go out and leave you here.
> But mind now, Conrad, what I say,
> Don't suck your thumb while I'm away.
> The great tall tailor always comes
> To little boys that suck their thumbs
> And ere they dream what he's about,
> He takes his great sharp scissors out
> And cuts their thumbs clean off,—and then,
> You know, they never grow again."
>
> Mamma had scarcely turn'd her back,
> The thumb was in, Alack! Alack!
>
> The door flew open, in he ran,
> The great, long red-legg'd scissor-man.
> Oh! children, see! the tailor's come
> And caught out little Suck-a-Thumb.
> Snip! Snap! Snip! They go so fast,
> That both his thumbs are off at last.

121

Mamma comes home; there Conrad stands
And looks quite sad, and shows his hands,—
"Ah!" said Mamma "I knew he'd come
To naughty little Suck-a-Thumb."

The story is illustrated with colored plates which show the thumbs being cut off. When Conrad sucks his thumb a face in the background is frowning; when his thumbs are gone the face is smiling. The story softens castration as a punishment (or treatment) for masturbating into a cutting-off of the thumbs for thumb-sucking.

This then was the social context in which Freud observed the "castration complex" in patients and came to believe it to be universal. Freud offered different views at different times about the relationship between threats of castration in childhood and castration anxiety in adult life. Here is an example from his writing:

> It is by no means a rare thing, for instance, for a little boy, who is beginning to play with his penis in a naughty way and is not yet aware that one must conceal such activities, to be threatened by a parent or nurse with having his penis or his sinful hand cut off. Parents will often admit this when they are asked, since they think they have done something useful in making such a threat; a number of people have a correct conscious memory of such a threat, especially if it was made at a somewhat later period. If the threat is delivered by the mother or some other female she usually shifts its performance on to the father—or the doctor. . . . But it is highly improbable that children are threatened with castration as often as it appears in the analyses of neurotics. We shall be satisfied by realising that the child puts a threat of this kind together in his imagination on the basis of hints, helped out by a knowledge that auto-erotic satisfaction is forbidden and under the impression of his discovery of the female genitals. (*Standard Edition*, *16*, p. 369)

Freud thought boys feel horror at girls' and women's lack of penises, which he maintains boys and girls construe as proof of girls' prior castration. Thus, he thought, boys who know that females lack penises are ready to believe their parents' threats of castration. He also suggests another basis for the castration complex: he says it is "an inherited endowment," a "phylogenetic heritage." He believes

> a child catches hold of this phylogenetic experience where his own experience fails him. He fills in the gaps in individual truth with prehistoric truth; he replaces occurrences in his own life by occurrences in the life of his ancestors. . . . (*Standard Edition*, *17*, p. 97)

Freud thought tribes in prehistory had practiced castration, which their descendants had consciously forgotten but unconsciously remembered, and that his patients' and everyone's castration fears are inherited *memories*. If so, we should all be fated by phylogeny to be paranoid, especially if we are males.

In the absence of hard evidence in support either of prehistorical castration or of phylogenetic memories, Freud's proposal, however interesting, is doubtful. Given available data about threatened and actual castration in Freud's time, it is a gratuitous explanation for castration fears in Freud's patients and others; for the same reason I find unnecessary his theory that boys' dread of castration derives from their discovery of the female genitals.

Psychoanalysis also understands a boy's fear of castration by his father to be based upon a projection of the boy's wish to castrate his father, i.e., the boy denies his own wish and displaces it onto his father. This view does not consider the possibility that a boy's unconscious wish to castrate his father might be a response to his father's behavior towards him.

Marx distinguished in human beings between "constant" or "fixed" drives and "relative" drives. He thought constant drives exist under all social conditions while relative ones occur in only some. Perhaps the "complexes" of psychoanalysis, like relative drives, are innate human possibilities, which become realized only in certain social settings.

The "castration complex," in my view, can be resolved into two components: a "castrat*ing* complex" and a "castrat*ed* complex." I doubt the *-ed* can exist without the *-ing*. But Freud regards only the *-ed* as a proper object for analysis. He seems to take threats of castration by doctors and parents as a universal given, as par for the course, and as not deserving scrutiny. However ruefully or sardonically he views the behavior of parents and his colleagues, he accepts it as a norm.

(3)

Consider Freud's report on "Little Hans," * a five-year-old boy whom he analyzed. Hans was refusing to go out into the street because he was afraid of horses and particularly of a horse biting him.

Freud ascribes to Hans' father (a physician) and mother qualities which the facts he presents clearly contradict. Frued says:

> His parents were both among my closest adherents, and they had agreed that in bringing up their first child [Hans] they would use no more coercion than might be absolutely necessary. . . . And, as the child developed . . . the experiment of letting him grow up and express himself *without being intimidated* went on satisfactorily. (*Standard Edition, 10*, p. 6)

> The education given him by his parents . . . consisted essentially in the omission of our usual educational sins. (*Ibid.*, p. 103)

In fact, Hans' parents bullied him and repeatedly lied to him.

On a visit to a zoo with his father Hans found access to the sheep blocked by a rope. Hans said it would be quite easy to slip under it; his father told him that "respectable people didn't

---

* For a fuller critique of Freud's analysis of "Little Hans" along lines similar to mine, see Fromm, Narváez, and others, 1968.

124

crawl under the rope" and "*a policeman might come along and take one off*" (p. 40).

Hans' father took notes about Hans and discussed them with Freud. Reporting this material, Freud writes that Hans

> was looking on intently while his mother undressed before going to bed. "What are you staring like that for?" she asked.
> *Hans:* "I was only looking to see if you'd got a widdler [*wiwimacher* in the original, i.e., penis] too."
> *Mother:* "Of course. Didn't you know that?" (pp. 9–10)

Both parents sustained this lie a few times. Later, when Hans' father tells him his mother and baby sister lack "widdlers," without telling him that or why his parents had previously lied to him, Hans refuses to believe his father's new information (p. 32). Freud explains Hans' disbelief on the grounds that the new truth was bound "to have aroused his castration complex" (p. 36). I think it simpler to assume that his parents' statements confused and frightened him, and that he found it hard to grant his mother had no "widdler," because this meant granting both his parents had told him lies. At four he still had not seen either of his parents' genitals.

When his baby sister was born he was three and a half. Freud reports the father wrote on the day of delivery:

> *Naturally* he has often been told during the last few days that the stork is going to bring a little girl or a little boy; and he *quite rightly* connected the unusual sounds of groaning with the stork's arrival. (p. 10)

Freud says about Hans:

> When he was three and a half his mother found him with his hand on his penis. She threatened him in these words: "If you do that, I shall send for Dr. A. to cut off your widdler. And then what'll you widdle with?" (pp. 7–8)

Hans' mother threatened to abandon him before he was four for being "naughty" (p. 45). This passage from the father's notes refers to another episode:

Hans: "But I don't put my hand to my widdler anymore."
I: "But you still want to."
Hans: "Yes, I do. But wanting's not doing, and doing's not wanting."
I: "Well, but to prevent your wanting to, this evening you're going to have a bag to sleep in." (p. 31)

Freud attributes Hans' phobia to

> the fear of impending castration. . . . His fear that a horse would bite him can, without any forcing, be given the full sense of a fear that a horse would bite off his genitals, would castrate him. (*Standard Edition, 20,* p. 108)

He seems to presume Hans' "castration complex" would have developed without the threat of castration when he says:

> Children construct this danger for themselves. . . . (*Standard Edition, 10,* p. 8n)

Freud neither draws attention to the parents' threats (except for the threat of castration) or lies nor considers them in his formulation of what was the matter with Hans.

We lack adequate data, I think, to be able to construct reliably a new theory of why Hans feared being bitten by horses. But we have enough to see that Freud disregarded at least certain parts of Hans' parents' behavior which could frighten and confuse a little boy.

Ideologies are ideas that serve as weapons for social interests. The castrat*ing* beliefs, threats, and practices I have sketched here represent the leading edge of nineteenth-century familial *ideologies.* They reflect and protect the existing power structure: fathers on top, women and children far below. And no one must masturbate. In masturbation a child finds delight by, for, in, and from himself or herself. He or she feels free for a fleeting moment from a need for external authority. It therefore can be, as Sartre has said, a dangerous act. Possibly, this is why the Victorian and Bismarckian world feared it so much.

The breeding ground for familial ideologies is the family. The nineteenth-century family (like many today) was a *factory* for authoritarian ideologies. It implanted its patterns of relations as patterns of mind upon its members.

Psychoanalysis, * by what it has failed to say about masturbation, the position of women and children, and the persecution of children by parents, has unwittingly conserved ideologies of its time; it has acquiesced in certain parts of the social status quo. To this day it has still not unequivocally freed masturbation from the stigma of being, especially in children, a mark of neurosis. Formerly psychoanalysis regarded masturbation as a possible cause of neurosis.

Freud, in dealing with persecution by parents of children, does not see it (Schreber), or sees it but does not see it as persecution ("Little Hans"), or does not explore it (Laius, the "castrat*ing* complex") or challenge it (the "castrat*ing* complex").

It has become fashionable in certain circles to tweak Freud for not calling into question the authoritarian family and political structures of his time and place. What of his followers? The psychoanalytic movement, * especially in its training institutes, still reflects to varying degrees in different countries the patriarchal family structure of the nineteenth-century middle-European bourgeoisie. Certain psychoanalysts originally justified this on the grounds of political expedience—a small embattled cadre of daring thinkers in unfriendly environs needed a closely knit, tightly run authoritarian framework. I do not think such a stronghold is needed now (I doubt it ever was). And the price paid for it, in the loss of radical ideas and thinkers, is high.

---

* When I speak of psychoanalysis or of the psychoanalytic movement, I am *not* referring to people like Erich Fromm, Karen Horney, R. D. Laing, and Harry Stack Sullivan; they have put forth views compatible with those I express here.

Models of the mind and systems of child development, like economic and political philosophies, cannot be understood if their social origins are obscured. States of mind correspond, however loosely, to their social contexts, theories about states of mind to *their* social contexts, and theories about relations between states of mind and social contexts to *their* social contexts. What all individuals, including theorists of the mind, are conscious of is partly determined by what their social situations *allow* them to be conscious of.

From the start, psychoanalysis and psychiatry, at every step, in theory and practice, have demystified and repudiated *and* protected and acquiesced in widespread ideologies.

I see psychoanalysis as generally *more* aware and *more* critical of widely believed ideologies than other psychotherapies.

No group of persons, lay or professional, is immune to the ideologizing influences of its social context. The authoritarian, patriarchal nineteenth-century family was one of the social conditions in which psychoanalysis developed and which it has sometimes seemed to embody. It has tended not to criticize certain tyrannies to which this family gave rise.

Schreber's cosmology—a male God atop a hierarchy of accomplices, deputies, and servants—seems to be a celestial projection of the scenario of his family of origin *and* of many families of his time. Anyone brought up in this type of family who learned to live successfully with its rules and roles, its premises and practices, would not be likely to see it as the source of someone else's feelings of persecution. This may be why, for fifty years after Schreber published his *Memoirs,* no one thought to connect his suffering with his father's attitudes toward children.

I have placed Freud's theory of paranoia within what I think is its relevant ideological setting, shown that the theory bypasses the issue of parents' persecution of children, and questioned the relation between some of Freud's data and his conclusions. This does not mean that I regard his conclusions as invalid. On the contrary, I think his theory has great explanatory power, given the data with which it deals, and that it has helped toward understanding regions of many people's minds. Also, Freud's followers have modified his theory of paranoia to make it more flexible and to allow it to cover more patterns of thought seen as paranoid. (See, for instance, Melanie Klein, 1948, pp. 282–310; Robert Waelder, 1951; W. R. D. Fairbairn, 1956; and many others.) But the revisions of Freud's original theory do not deal, nor could they deal, without being revised themselves, with data from Schreber's father's writings. This is because, in their idioms and ideas, they are concerned with relations between objects or structures, not persons: a sadistic "part-object" or a punitive "superego" is *not* a cruel father or a transformed memory of one.

IX

THE PERSECUTION OF *THAT*

A most important development in the theory of persons in the past twenty-five years has been, in my view, the growing awareness that no one can adequately be understood isolated from his or her social context. Each person's experience and behavior, whether he be considered sane or mad, are intelligible, at least partly, as responses to others' behavior, past and present, toward and around him.

The language and labels psychiatrists use, however, are still oriented toward "ill" or "deviant" individuals. Psychiatric nosology classifies individuals psychiatrists see as disturbed, but lacks categories for labeling the interpersonal situations that may be disturbing them. We need suitable idioms, schemas, and models with which to think about the effects on persons of social contexts—families, schools, churches, factories, and clubs—and about relations between micro-social small groups and their macro-social context—Society as a whole.

Psychoanalysis presupposes, at least in theory, a person's feelings of persecution to be partly or wholly occasioned by instinctually or phylogenetically determined fantasies. Of course, many psychoanalysts know the stories of childhood persecution they hear from patients are valid. But this, however endearing, is unsatisfactory if they have no theory by which to explain how past persecution can occasion certain strange experiences later on.

In this chapter I shall discuss connections between events that occur inside people and those that happen between people. I shall ply between the intra- and interpersonal levels, never straying far from the Schreber case. What I say here may shed light on the situations of some persons other than Schreber, regarded as paranoid or schizophrenic. I also suggest some ways to think about links between patterns of experience and behavior in individuals and patterns of events in their families of origin.

Consider someone who regards certain events in his mind (thoughts, feelings, perceptions, memories, etc.) as bad, mad, obscene, impure, dirty, or dangerous. If he wishes to consider himself good, sane, decent, pure, clean, and safe, he needs to adopt tactics to deal with those events, when or before they appear to consciousness. One can flee dangers or "bad" elements in the world around oneself; one avoids them by removing oneself from them. But flight is of no avail here; one cannot withdraw one's mind from itself.

There is a feasible and often used ploy: pretend to oneself that certain events in one's mind do not occur, i.e., withdraw *consciousness* from them. Out of consciousness does not mean out of mind; it only seems so. As objects in the external world do not disappear when we turn our backs on them, so events in the mind do not stop occurring because we look away from them. And, while outside awareness, they often undergo changes.

Freud used several terms to name the operation of putting or keeping events out of awareness, e.g., to repress *(verdrängen)*, to disavow *(verleugnen)*, and to reject *(verwerfen)*; and a few to imply partial unawareness, e.g., to condemn *(verurteilen)* and to negate *(verneinen)*. René Laforgue, a French psychoanalyst, used a term that is translated into English as, to scotomize, i.e., to make oneself blind to; many psychoanalysts speak of repudiating or denying events. All these terms represent means whereby one disaffiliates oneself from possibilities of one's own mind. I use these words interchangeably since I find it hard in practice to distinguish from each other the operations to which they refer. Here, for convenience, I rely on one of them, repression. By means of repression a mind tries to expropriate from itself elements it thinks are inappropriate; it changes "bad-me" into "not-me."

Repression is probably a complex maneuver involving operations, occurring simultaneously, that (1) define certain thoughts as bad, (2) condemn the thoughts, (3) push and keep the thoughts out of awareness, and (4) push and keep (1), (2), and (3) also out of awareness. For more elaboration on this see Laing, 1971, pp. 97–99, 104–116. John Lilly (1970) expresses a similar idea in computer idiom when he says that much of the "storage material" and "programs" in one's mind are invisible to oneself; he suggests that a "program" may dictate that all or some "storage" must be distorted before appearing to consciousness, or must be hidden from consciousness altogether. And another program may distort or hide *that* program.

This may be why certain people who believe they never think, thought, or could think "bad" thoughts generally also believe they do not, did not, and could not need rules to prohibit themselves from thinking the thoughts. They suppose they are just "naturally" right-thinking.

Repression is one, perhaps the most basic, of a class of operations we perform upon our experience to normalize it, i.e., to manicure it to fit our view and our view of others' views of what is sane, clean, decent, right, pure, safe, good, etc. Psychoanalysts call the class of operations defenses. Defenses face in two directions at once: they serve both as defenses *from* and as defenses *of*.

1. The defenses *of* consciousness keep consciousness defended *from* "bad" thoughts.

2. The defenses *of* "bad" thoughts keep them defended
from consciousness.

The word "defenses" in each sentence refers to the same set
of operations seen from two sides. Defenses, by keeping consciousness and "bad" thoughts apart from each other, tend to
protect each from the other.

The defenses of which psychoanalysts speak are operations
one performs upon one's *own* experience. These operations are
often not enough to ensure that one will remain pure. Suppose
I wish to keep certain of my possibilities, which I fear, apart
from my consciousness; it would be helpful, perhaps necessary,
for me to abolish reminders of them in *other* people's behavior.
You must stop acting in a way that recalls to me my impure
wishes. So must everyone, if I could have my way. If you or
they do not stop upsetting me, I shall have to remove you, or
them, or myself.

I shall call the class of acts by which one operates on others'
behavior and experience, in order to defend oneself against
"bad" events in one's own mind, *transpersonal* defenses; in so
doing, I am using a term and a concept already put forth by
Laing (1965, p. 349 and 1971, p. 13).

We lay our defenses in depth. If I wish to conceal a "bad"
thought from myself, I usually conceal the thought, the act of
concealing it, the rule requiring its concealment, and the awareness that I am concealing anything. If I wish to remove from
other people's behavior and experience reminders of what I am
concealing from myself and if I also wish to keep concealed
from myself that I am concealing something, I can suppose that
I am acting upon other people not for my sake, but for *theirs*.
I transpose the locus of the "improvement" I wish to bring
about from inside me to inside others. My efforts are for their
sakes only.

Now I am in this position: wherever I see "badness" I must
destroy it, thinking I do it on behalf of others. Since what I

am trying to destroy in others are really my own suppressed, unfulfilled possibilities, which will live until I die, my work is lifelong. The cost of unawareness is eternal vigilance.

In order to make invisible to oneself "bad" events in the minds of other people, one must remove from other people's behavior signs of those events. Behavior reflects experience; therefore, if one needs or wishes to make oneself even safer, one should prevail upon the others not even to know such events do, ever did, or even could, occur in their minds. It is best to train people in "good" habits of mind when they are young. An ounce of prevention is worth a pound of cure.

Frequently Dr. Schreber advises parents to make their children unaware of their own experience, if it is of a sort he thinks is bad. He tells parents to stage this scene with their children, three to five years old, as a training exercise after punishing them; the aim is to induce the children to feel what he thinks they should.

> It is generally healthy for the sentiments if the child after each punishment, after he has recovered, is gently prodded (preferably by a third person) to offer to shake the hand of the punisher as a sign of a plea for forgiveness. . . . From then on everything should be forgotten.
>
> After this prodding has occurred a few times the child, feeling his duty, will freely approach the punisher. This ensures against the possibility of residual spiteful or bitter feelings and mediates the feeling of repentance (the next goal of punishment) and the benefit that results from it, and generally gives the child the healthy impression that he still owes the punisher something, not the other way around, even if maybe a word or a blow more than necessary should have befallen the child. Generally, any plea for love must come from the child, and only from the child. . . . If one forgets about the repentance process here one risks always that the main aim of each punishment, the true serious feeling of repentance, will not be reached but instead a kernel of bitter feeling will stay stuck in the depths of children's hearts. If one were to omit this procedure altogether one would

permit the punished child the right of anger against the punisher, which is certainly not consistent with an intelligent pedagogic approach. (1858, p. 142)

To clarify all Dr. Schreber's implicit premises here and other premises that these imply would take us off our course. Briefly, here are a few that are apparent:

Punishment of a child is proof of his guilt. Although punishment can be excessive, it can never be unwarranted. Its aim is to bring about an acknowledgment of guilt, which he calls repentance.

It is a child's duty, not his choice, to ask for forgiveness.

Only the punisher can forgive a punished child.

One acts in the light of what one sees. Each of these premises is a constraint by which Dr. Schreber limits his vision. He forces the child's view to fit his view of what the child's view should be. This he can do only by altering the child's experience. Any "spite," "bitterness," or "anger" the child feels toward his punisher must be repressed.

Repression, in the psychoanalytic view, is an *intra*personal defense built to ward off real, imagined, or fantasied harm. Freud said that a person represses experience if he fears it may lead him to act in ways for which he remembers (or imagines, or fantasies) he has been punished, or for which he perceives (or imagines, or fantasies) he will be punished. Repression can be the consequence of a *trans*personal maneuver. I am distinguishing one's operation upon another's experience (transpersonal) from one's operation upon one's own (intrapersonal).

A person (often a parent) orders another person (often a child) to forget thoughts, feelings, or acts that the first person cannot or will not allow in the other. This is standard practice in some relationships (especially in families with a schizophrenic offspring). If the first person's aim is to protect himself from experience of which he fears the other may remind him, if the other experiences too much, the order serves as a transpersonal *defense*. A transpersonal defense can be an *attack* on another person's experience, against which the other may in turn need to build a defense.

Dr. Schreber recommends a transpersonal maneuver in order to induce repression in a child. The maneuver could have served as a transpersonal defense for him if he feared *his un*-"repentant" feelings toward his parents. His son thought that someone might think God could resort to what I am calling transpersonal defenses:

> Whoever has taken the .trouble of reading the above attentively may spontaneously have thought that God Himself must have been or be in a precarious position, if the conduct of a single human being could endanger Him in any way and even if He Himself, if only in limited instances, could be enticed into a kind of *conspiracy against human beings who are fundamentally innocent.* (*Memoirs,* p. 59)

Later, he says he "had become a danger to God Himself" (*ibid.,* p. 75) and "God acts towards me in *self-defence*" (p. 177). In a postscript to his book he notes:

> God is a living Being and would Himself have to be ruled by egoistic motives, if other living beings existed who could endanger Him or in some way be detrimental to His interests. (pp. 251–252)

Is he ascribing operations to his father's mind, to explain his father's behavior, without naming him?

Possibly, many or all the defenses of psychoanalysis were originally formed in childhood against the attacks of adults who feared to be reminded by children of their own suppressed possibilities.

Let us call the person who *gen*erates paranoid states in others a paranoido*gen*ic person. He is, I believe, someone who persecutes or is persecuted by (it is hard to distinguish active from passive here) possibilities of his own being that he regards as bad and that he tries to destroy "in" others. Here is a recipe for it:

> Regard part of oneself, *That*, as bad (or mad, obscene, impure, dirty, dangerous, etc.).

> Fear That will destroy oneself if oneself does not destroy That.

> Destroy That in oneself by denying That is part of oneself.

> Deny the denial, that anything is denied, and the denial of the denial.

> Discover That in other people.

> Fear That in them will destroy them, others, or oneself if That is not destroyed.

> Adopt means to destroy That in them, even if this entails destroying the people in whom one has discovered That.

In order to be effective as a paranoidogenic person, it is best to have power over one's victim of a sort the victim cannot easily escape; inquisitor over heretic, hospital psychiatrist over involuntary mental patient, parent over child.

I believe Dr. Schreber to be a prime example of a paranoidogenic person.

(The term "That," as I am using it, is distinct from Georg Groddeck's "It" and Freud's "id." Groddeck's It [1961] is "some wondrous force" within man that "directs both what he himself does and what happens to him." It is that by which man is "lived" [pp. 18–19]. The It [1951] is the

> deepest nature and force of the man. It accomplishes everything that happens with and through and in the man. [p. 40]

Freud says [1933] about the id:

We call it a chaos, a cauldron full of seething excitations. We picture it as being open at its end to somatic influences, and as there taking up into itself instinctual needs which find their expression in it . . . It has no organization, produces . . . only a striving to bring about the satisfaction of the instinctual needs. [*Standard Edition, 22,* p. *73*]

Groddeck's It and Freud's id, unlike what I call That, are not socially determined in their being. They preexist social life, although social forces impinge upon them. All societies treat as That, in my sense, certain expressions both of Groddeck's It and Freud's id, but the ones a given society treats as That vary.)

Homosexual feelings and acts can be That, and often have been That in the West for at least the past fifteen centuries. Homosexuals have been put to death as heretics. Freud connected feelings of persecution with homosexual love; he may have correctly noticed they often *are* connected. But would they be linked as often or at all in a society that openly endorsed and valued homosexual love? Given the way active and suspected homosexuals have been and are persecuted, it is no surprise that "latent" homosexuals fear persecution. We could speak of a paranoidogenic *society*.

If someone feels persecuted by homosexual wishes, he may be remembering or perceiving real or threatened persecution for his wishes, whether or not he knows of his wishes or that or why he feels persecuted by them. Many adults, as children, experienced persons of the same sex, toward whom they expressed sexual desires, responding to them with anger or contempt—probably because of a fear of arousal of their *own* homosexual desires.

We can ask a question that seems unanswerable: if most of us learned to repress homosexual desires in infancy, why do more of us not feel persecuted?

Homosexuality, persecution, and what is called paranoia can dovetail hellishly. I have known a young man who was so terrified other men were thinking he wished to seduce them sexually that he *chose* to stop speaking and moving. In this way no one could "accuse" him of a seductive voice inflection or a "swishy" walk. His parents, annoyed that he was "not being sociable," brought him to a mental hospital where he was confined involuntarily. He was labeled a paranoid and catatonic schizophrenic and given electric shock, also against his will. The staff, mostly male, had reasoned that he "really" wanted a man to rape him and that if a male doctor "charged him up" electrically and made him convulse (an "orgasm equivalent"), he would at once satisfy both his "unconscious" erotic wishes and the punishment for them he "unconsciously" desired. I wonder in how many societies someone could tie himself and be tied into such a tangle over the issue of homosexual love.

Homosexuals in "top security" positions in government or in large corporations, especially before about ten years ago, were sometimes persecuted in a curious way. If the boss discovered their homosexuality, he might ask them to leave their jobs on the grounds that they were "security risks": they were considered vulnerable to blackmail by someone who threatened to reveal their homosexuality. They may in fact have been susceptible to blackmail, mainly because of the threat to their jobs if their homosexuality were disclosed, while their jobs were vulnerable because of the supposed possibility of blackmail.

Homosexual thoughts compose one class of mental events that can occasion persecution (and paranoia). *Any* possibilities of mind that minds choose to condemn as bad and to destroy can be That. The wish to masturbate was That in most of the West for one hundred and fifty years and still is in certain circles. "Self-abuse" still occasions both persecution and paranoia. Dr. Schreber, the father, and possibly his son too, seemed to regard anger at a parent as That.

Many people, in order to maintain their mental equilibrium, try to control events in some minds other than their own.*

---

* People considered obsessional try to attain the same aim by arranging events "correctly" in the material world. A person who is either obsessional or paranoidogenic can be both, though he need not be.

But certain persons, not necessarily regarded clinically as psychotic, in order to keep their balance, lay down parameters to govern others' states of mind to such extent and in such ways that the others cannot remain sane. In fact, they persecute others, often without seeing what they do as persecution. A favorite analogy of Gregory Bateson, an American ethnologist is: a car can break down either by not being able to move or, while continuing to move, by suffocating motorists behind it in clouds of exhaust fumes. This second type of "breakdown" seems characteristic of parents of certain persons seen as insane.

The theory I have been outlining here, insofar as it depends upon the assumption of unconscious mental events, is hard to illustrate with real-life or clinical examples. We cannot experience directly events occurring in other people's minds. We can observe someone's behavior, but not the experience or the operations upon the experience we may believe underlie the behavior. If the operations are not evident to the person in whose mind they occur, he cannot tell us of them.

I know of no certain criteria by which to ascertain the operation of repression (as an intrapsychic operation). It is invisible; its presence can only be inferred from the absence of the conscious experience of the events upon which it is presumably operating. One becomes aware of its existence within oneself only *after* having undone it.

The same is so for all the defenses of psychoanalysis, the intrapsychic steps in my "recipe" for paranoidogenicity, and all the elements against which these operations are formed. I have never heard (nor should I expect to hear) anyone say he is teaching his children to be "good" in order that *he* remain sane, because he fears that if they were "bad," they would remind him of "bad" elements he was repressing in himself, which if unrepressed would threaten his sanity. Some of or all these steps are themselves repressed.

By supplying inferences and constructions, I can interlace available evidence about Dr. Schreber, the father, into illustrations of my theory of paranoidogenicity. It seems impossible to me to prove a theory that partly depends upon ascribing to someone's mind operations of which he is unaware.

A possible example of a That for Dr. Schreber: attacks of melancholia. Niederland (1960) has found in a book by Dr. Schreber

> a brief case history entitled "Confessions of One Who Had Been Insane" *(Geständnis eines Wahnsinnig Gewesenen)*. This report which Schreber attributes to a chance acquaintance he made during his early travels, is filled with vague allusions to attacks of melancholia, morbid brooding, and tormenting criminal impulses. In its veiled language the account reads like an autobiographical record. . . . (p. 494)

Niederland concludes that the father "as an adolescent . . . was a rather disturbed young man."

Consider Dr. Schreber's view on "ill-temper, morose or sulky forms of mind" in children two to eight years old:

> Once the sky becomes overcast, the cloud is harder to break. A well-timed, strong word, a menacing lightning flash from afar, which strikes if necessary, clears the sky again most quickly. It is very important and forms the foundation of the disposition for life, that the child should regard every fit of ungrounded ill-temper, morose or sulky forms of mind as something forbidden. . . . Conversely, if one gives the state of mind free rein and waits passively until it has ceased raging, its strength grows until it is unconquerable. But we all know what kind of *life-endangering daemon* the initially innocuous mood is in its surreptitiously advancing steps of development. (1858, p. 130)

On "depressive emotions" in children eight to sixteen:

> We should best apply the general rule here: all ignoble and immoral as well as other depressive emotions (especially groundless sadness and anger, sourness and solemnness) must all be suffocated in their seed right away by immediate diversion or direct suppression. . . . We have to pay special attention to the

surly or irritable sentiments of some children, which appear as
the result not only of a temporary physical ill-feeling but as a
seeping poison of the soul. These demand in the beginning a
gentler kind of treatment such as keeping all food from the
child. . . . More dangerous is the luckily rarer, silent, biting,
tenacious anger or sadness. . . . One has to feel out the rotten
spots by means of intense help; otherwise they eat away and
the roots get so strong that this process will continue indefi-
nitely. It is important that no traces of this stay in the depths
because all, even the deeply dormant weeds of the soul, will in
early or later life easily become dangerous if they receive new
nourishment to infest from any directions. The *insane asylums*
would deliver many proofs of this if one could follow the individual histories of the sufferings of the unhappy ones down to
the last traces of the roots. (*Ibid.*, p. 241)

I think it likely that the father feared "rotten spots" in his
own soul. Perhaps "deeply dormant weeds" had once threatened
his view of himself as sane. He could not, I suppose, admit he
ever had or still feared them, because to admit the fear would
mean to admit the possibility of That within himself that he
feared. He withdraws his consciousness from *his* "seeping poison" and thereby comes to believe that "no traces of this stay
in the depths" of himself. And he denies that he so withdraws
his consciousness.

His soaring toward high moral ideals can be seen to be his
way of denying or flying from the threat of *his* "depressive
emotions"; in so doing he may be employing, in the idiom of
Melanie Klein and Donald Winnicott, the English psychoanalysts, a "manic defence." (See Winnicott, 1958, pp. 129–
144.)

What he fears reappears for him as a possible threat to the
sanity of adolescents, not his own. He must destroy That in
them by "immediate diversion or direct suppression" of *their*
consciousness or even by starving them—"a gentler kind of
treatment." Since he may have been subject to brooding in his

143

own adolescence, it is fitting that it is adolescents whose mental health he thinks is similarly endangered.

Uncannily, he achieved with his sons here too exactly what he wished to avoid. One son's hospital records (Baumeyer, 1956) say that he suffered from "deep emotional depression" and was "very moody"; he frequently talked of suicide and tried it a few times. And the father's elder son killed himself. We do not know how the father brought about in his sons exactly what he feared, but we can guess. Maybe his sons saw him depressed or fighting off depressions and imitated or identified with his state of mind.

Possibly, the father in fact went mad. Alfons Ritter, who wrote a doctoral dissertation about the father, says:

> Towards the end of the 1850s [he would have been about fifty] Schreber had a serious and unfortunate accident—a heavy iron ladder fell on his head in the gymnasium—which left him suffering from chronic headaches (it was not possible to find an exact medical diagnosis), which often kept him in the house for half a day at a time. He . . . lived in constant fear of insanity . . . the question as to whether the blow of the ladder or a bad nervous breakdown caused the pain . . . was the subject of contemporary debate. (1936, p. 14)

Mathematicians call a property in a given series hereditary when, if it belongs to any element in the series, the next element also possesses it. (Any hereditary property possessed by zero must belong to all finite numbers; any hereditary property possessed by Adam must belong to all men. Mathematicians' use of the term "hereditary" is logically more basic than biologists' usage.) "Bad" thoughts or states of mind may be hereditary, in this sense, in certain family lineages, at least over limited time spans. If parents persecute what they think are "bad" thoughts or "bad" mental states in their offspring, because their parents persecuted the same "badness" in them as children, and if their offspring when they grow up do the same to their children,

144

that "badness" may be regarded as hereditary in that family line. "Badness," like bad genes, has a transindividual existence, being passed on, often unawares, from parents to children.

What is called paranoia or what could be called paranoidogenicity (the condition of inducing or causing paranoia in others) may be "inherited," not in the genes, but by each generation teaching the next one to fear certain possibilities of mind. The study has barely begun of the means of transmission of "bad" thoughts and mental states, how lines of transmission spontaneously begin or end, and how they could be deliberately interrupted by outside interventions.

We are all victims or beneficiaries, depending upon one's biases, of programs laid down by humans long before us. It may be as hard for a given individual to bring about change in the whole system of premises governing his experience and that of his social group as to alter the grammar of his native language.

PARANOIA AND PERSECUTION

We must remember that every "mental" symptom is a veiled cry of anguish. Against what? Against oppression, or what the patient experiences as oppression. The oppressed speak in a million tongues. . . . They make use of all the well-tried language of illness and suffering and constantly add new tongues newly created for special occasions. They need these marvellously complicated linguistic devices, for, at a single stroke they must reveal and conceal themselves.

What of the psychiatrist or of others who wish to help ouch a person? Should they amplify the dissent and help the oppressed shout it aloud? Or should they strangle the cry and re-oppress the fugitive slave? This is the psychiatric therapist's moral dilemma.

Thomas Szasz, 1968

Many people feel persecuted but no one ever feels paranoid. Paranoia is not an experience; it is an attribution one person makes about another. It is a judgment that someone else's feelings of persecution do not refer to anything real. The person feeling persecuted believes what he feels persecuted by *is* real. Of course, someone may say about himself "I'm paranoid" but in doing so he adopts a position of otherness in relation to his

147

own experience. He becomes, as it were, both another person, looking at and judging his experience "objectively," and an object, looked at and judged.

The view that someone's, even one's own, feelings of persecution are invalid can be incorrect. I think many people whom psychiatrists call paranoid are or have been persecuted and know it, but they do not recognize their real persecutors or how they have been persecuted. To call them paranoid, which presupposes they are not really persecuted, but imagine it, is false and misleading.

Consider a matrix with two columns and two rows, yielding four possibilities:

One is not persecuted and	Knows it	Does not know it
	1. This state is regarded as normal.	2. i.e., one thinks one is persecuted when one is not. Psychiatrists believe people they call paranoid are in this state.
One is persecuted and	3. One is a knowing victim.	4. This state has no name.

The first position is "normal." The second is ascribed by psychiatrists to people they call paranoid. What of the last two, especially the fourth?

There is no term in psychiatric usage, or in English, for "is persecuted without knowing it." Since there is no name for this condition, one can suffer from it without risk of being labeled. I think it is a prevalent condition. I believe many of the "healthy" siblings of people considered paranoid or schizophrenic endure it.

148

(Note: When I say "is persecuted," I also mean *has been* persecuted. Some persons, persecuted by parents in childhood, are also persecuted by them in adulthood. Some unwittingly find or induce others to persecute them, often in ways remarkably similar to their childhood experience. And many, like Schreber, are persecuted by memories of past persecution.)

What is clinically called paranoia is often the partial realization—as through a glass darkly—that one has been or is persecuted. One may never have realized it before. "Paranoid" thoughts can be *images* of events which originally, days or decades earlier, were seen, heard, felt, smelled, or tasted.

William James, the American philosopher and psychologist, used to say that the question should be asked about any theory: what practical difference would it make to suppose it to be true? Many psychoanalysts and some psychiatrists think certain persons become schizophrenic or paranoid as the result of a lifting of repression. But a repression of what? Of homosexual love, of memories of being persecuted by other people, of both, of neither, of something else? It makes a difference what one believes. Many therapists explicitly aim treatment at *increasing* or restoring repression, not lifting it more. If I am right in my theory, to restore repression could mean to move people from the category of being persecuted and knowing it to being persecuted and not knowing it. I wonder if therapists would wish to increase their patients' repression if they thought this were the type of repression involved.

Some people cannot identify their persecutors or the methods of persecution, because their persecutors have not let them. The persecutors may persuade or force their victims to see their persecution as love, especially if the persecutors are the victims' parents, siblings, spouses, or children. The persecutors can lie more easily if they believe their own lies. If they see their persuasion or force also as love, they may try to convince their victims of this too.

In order to enhance one's paranoidogenicity, i.e., one's ability

149

to induce paranoia in others, a few ploys are especially helpful: regard one's persecution as love. If one's victims see one's persecution as persecution, consider their view as evidence of how much they need one's "love." Account for one's victims' resistance to one's persecution as an expression of That—as heresy, mental illness (e.g., paranoia), or, in Dr. Schreber's terms, as self-will or wilfulness. In the face of resistance, sustain one's persecution (or "love") with more zeal. Here is a schema that is simpler than family life in vivo ever is:

Parent persecutes Child.

Parent sees Parent's persecution as love.

Child sees Parent's persecution as persecution.

Child may or may not see that Parent sees his persecution of Child as love: usually he does not.

Parent wants Child to love, honor, and obey Parent, for Child's sake. If Child does not, Parent must force Child to, for Child's sake.

The more Child sees Parent's persecution as persecution, the more Parent persecutes Child and sees his persecution as love.

Child tries to conceal that he sees Parent's persecution as persecution, and to conceal that he is concealing something.

Parent tells Child: "Dishonesty is wicked. I will punish you, for your own good, if you lie."

(A variation is: "You *cannot* hide your feelings from me." I am distinguishing "You should not hide your feelings from me" from "You *cannot* hide your feelings from me." The first is an order; the second an attribution that masks an order. The second is like the hypnotist's induction and is a stronger technique of control, probably because the order is hidden. For more discussion of this point see Laing, 1971, pp. 78–81, and Haley, 1963, pp. 20–40.)

Child sees that Parent will persecute Child most if Parent sees that Child sees Parent's persecution as persecution, and is concealing that he is, and is concealing that there is something he is concealing.

Child conceals from *himself* that he sees that Parent persecutes him, and conceals from *himself* that there is something he is concealing.

If this schema or one like it summarizes some of what has occurred between some "paranoid" people, when they were children, and their parents, it would shed light on why they so mistrust others. It would also explain Robert Knight's finding (1940) that ascribing homosexual wishes to a "paranoid" patient "not only does not relieve the patient but often makes him more paranoid than ever" (quoted by Macalpine and Hunter, 1955, p. 23).

I deduce from my study of Schreber's father's ideas that this situation, or one like it, existed between father and son.

No theory can ever be exposed to all possible relevant tests. It is best to ask about a theory not "Is it true?" but "What is its probability in the light of the available evidence?" and "What explanatory power can it bring to bear upon the evidence?"

Philosophers of science have repeatedly shown that more than one theory can always be placed on a given collection of data. In the case of competing theories we should ask: "Which one fits the facts better?" My theory and Freud's about Schreber's feelings of persecution do not exclude each other. I believe my theory encompasses more of the facts at hand than Freud's.

The writings of the father and son show that what the father saw as love, his son saw as persecution. Note the opposite values each gives to "rays." I have already quoted in another context the father's statement:

> Once the childish mind is completely penetrated by *love* and *respect* and all the warm *rays* which gush forth from them, the

151

will of the child is ruled more and more from this perspective and is led gently towards the pure and noble direction. (1858, p. 235)

Son says:

> In itself a state of affairs must be considered contrary to the Order of the World in which the *rays* serve mainly to *inflict damage* on the body of a single human being or to play tricks with the objects with which he is occupied—such harmless miracles have become particularly frequent latterly. (*Memoirs*, p. 132)

> Naturally I am referring only to *my own case*, that is to say a case in which God entered into continual contact by *rays* with a single human being, a contact which could no longer be severed and which therefore was contrary to the Order of the World. (*Ibid.*, p. 153)

Again, father and son use the same word, *Strahlen*, translated here as "rays."

Schreber feels harassed by God's attraction to him and would like God to withdraw from him, a perfectly intelligible wish in view of his father's behavior toward him as a child. He is not attract*ed* to God, as Freud thought; he is attract*ive*, and would like not to be. It is not "I love him" that bothers him, but "He loves me."

Baumeyer (1956) in his report of Schreber's hospital records says that Schreber "often declared that he had to put up a strong resistance *against* 'the homosexual *love* of certain persons'" (p. 63).

The following passage of the father shows how an able persecutor controlled his victims in the name of truth, openheartedness, and courage; it illustrates the last steps of my schema:

> . . . If one does not secure in the child's heart adherence to truth by imprinting of a *holy fear* of each glimmer of untruth, how can one wonder when later in life, with thousands of temptations to lie frequently demanding one's whole power to

resist, the domination of the lie spreads its rule, already having been prepared in youth. . . . *The child should be permeated by the feeling of the impossibility of locking up something in his heart knowingly and permanently from you. Without this unconditional openheartedness, any upbringing will lack a safe foundation.* But to get there an additional condition must be fulfilled. You have to come to the help of the child so that he can take in and secure the courage often necessary to hold strictly to the truth; this means in the case of a freely offered, open and full confession of guilt the guilt must be judged and punished recognisably more mildly, taking account of the openness, but in the opposite case the guilt is punished onefold, the untruth connected with it is punished tenfold. (1858, pp. 144–145)

Big Brother was incarnate long before George Orwell wrote *1984.*

Many psychiatrists and psychoanalysts have said that the people they call schizophrenic suffer from an inability to distinguish "I" from "not-I," that they lack "ego boundaries." I suggest that some of these people have been taught by their families they should not, or cannot, live with an "I," as Schreber's father apparently taught him. Note that Dr. Schreber does not say children should not keep things from their parents; he says they should be *"permeated by the feeling of the impossibility"* of it, i.e., they must feel that they *cannot.*

Although I part company here with prevalent views about paranoia, my position finds echoes in others' writings. O. H. Mowrer (1953), an American psychologist, said:

> It would seem more natural, certainly more parsimonious, to interpret paranoid delusions as projections of dissociated conscience than as projections of repressed homosexuality. (pp. 88–89)

I should have substituted "memories or perceptions of persecution" for "conscience."

W. Ronald D. Fairbairn (1956), the Scottish psychoanalyst, who couches his analysis of Schreber, the son, in object-relations idiom, implies that Schreber may have had "a sadistic superego," composed of multiple "internalized" "bad objects," which, when Schreber went mad, "disintegrated" into those "part objects" "with the consequent release of a host of internal persecutors," which he "defensively projected into the external world" (p. 119). I should have chosen to speak of memories of real persecution by others or transforms of those memories rather than of "part objects."

I agree with Harold Searles (1965), the American psychoanalyst, when he writes:

> The schizophrenic patient's so frequent delusion of being magically "influenced" by outside forces (radar, electricity, or what-not) is rooted partially in the fact of his responding to unconscious processes in people about him—people, who being unaware of these processes, will not and cannot help him to realise that the "influence" comes from a non-magical, interpersonal force. (p. 192)

I see many of Dr. Schreber's acts toward children as persecution and so would many people today. But he did not, nor as far as we know did his contemporaries or many people who lived years later. He felt love motivated his conduct toward children. He says to parents:

> All your dealings with the child, all your influence upon it must be founded upon love, i.e. on true, pure, and sensible love. It is not love if you do this or that for the child, if you undertake this or that with the child, and more thorough examination reveals this as proceeding exclusively from your own self-love, or from your own fancifulness, vanity, striving to entertain and amuse yourself by means of the child, or from other subordinate purposes. (1858, p. 131)

Dr. L. M. Politzer (1862), a professional colleague, says about Dr. Schreber in an obituary that he had "a heart full of *most devoted love*, prepared to live and die for his task" (p. 2). Politzer is probably echoing Dr. Schreber's view of himself.

Alfons Ritter (1936) speaks of Dr. Schreber's being "moved by" "the *philanthropic* ethic of a great human being" and a "*love* of the people" (p. 17); he says Dr. Schreber was "*full of love*" (p. 23). Talking of Dr. Schreber's household, Ritter writes:

> The children never had the feeling of being constantly nagged. Everything moved in the sphere of *freedom* and therefore with an unquestioning trust. (p. 14)

If Dr. Schreber and others saw as love what his son saw as persecution, another issue comes into view: can one be sure that what one sees as love or persecution *is* love or persecution? The concepts of love and persecution are indeterminate. One's decision to regard certain kinds of behavior as love or persecution is not the sort of decision that can be reached, as far as I can see, by existing methods of science. The decision is subjective and is influenced largely by what we might call one's sensitivity, which in turn is partly a product of one's prior programming. A man is tying a child to a bed: persecution or love?

What one sees to be going on with a given person or relationship between persons depends not only upon what is going on but upon one's styles of perceiving or interpreting. There are few, if any, reliable criteria for deciding whose view is more "correct" in a social situation where individuals' perspectives upon it differ.

I have suggested the person seen as paranoid may not be imagining he is persecuted and that possibly, in fact, he has been or is persecuted by other persons. The hypothesis needs revision: he *experiences* as persecution what he himself may have previously experienced differently *and* what others, including his persecutors, their other victims, e.g., his siblings, and his doctors often do not experience as persecution. They may see his feelings of persecution as invalid. He may experience their failure to see his feelings as valid as itself a form of persecution.

This complicates research that would aim to test my hypothesis; what a given investigator sees as going on in a given interpersonal situation depends partly upon his ability to see what is going on, i.e., upon what might loosely be called his perceptiveness.

The person seen as ill may see what is happening around him differently from anyone else. The others' disposition not to acknowledge that his vision could be valid may be a necessary, though insufficient, predisposing element in his so-called paranoia. If we say he is the seeing man in the country of the blind—however dim or blurred his vision—and they say he is mad, who is "right"? They say he is less conscious than they of "reality"; that is his "illness," they say. Dostoevsky once said, "I swear gentlemen, that to be *too conscious* is an illness— a real thoroughgoing illness."

Martti Siirala, a Finnish psychiatrist, maintains that many so-called symptoms of schizophrenia might be occasioned by an inherited predisposition, not of the patient, but of the people around him, to combat unusual tendencies in him that disturb their view of reality (1961, p. 73). If Siirala were right, geneticists would need to revise their premises about what it is that runs in families of schizophrenics. Siirala's views are highly speculative and would be hard to test. I mention them to jog loose any too-fixed, too-pat assumptions you may have.

Paranoia (*para*, beside, beyond + *nous*, mind) means literally the state of being beside, or out of, one's mind. I first became puzzled as a small child by the expression "out of his mind." Where, I wondered, is someone who is out of his mind and where is his mind "out of" which he is. The literal meaning of the phrase is absurd. Someone can become conscious of parts of his mind that he has never been conscious of before and lose consciousness of those parts of which he has been conscious. But no one, ever, can become conscious of any events except those in his mind. Perceptions are given to us to experience because, and only because, events originating outside us occasion events in our minds. Even "out of the body" experiences, where someone sees his body from a vantage point seemingly outside his body, must correspond to events in the experiencer's mind.*

In everyday speech, to say someone is "out of his mind" connotes that he is "out of" or unaware of those elements of his mind that fit certain prevailing views of rationality and is preoccupied with elements that do not. To be rational means to perceive reality and to draw proper inferences from it. Our culture defines "reality" differently from others, and within our culture official fashions of defining it have changed drastically. Some "heretics" of yesteryear (such as Galileo) are now heroes. Other individuals, persecuted when alive, and later made saints by the Church, now are seen as psychotic. Many people nowadays would consider Schreber's feelings of persecution valid if connected with his childhood. But it is unlikely that many people, if anyone, would have thought so when he was alive. If he saw the truth when he said he was persecuted (without seeing by whom or how), he was partly "in" his mind. The label "paranoia" would be, in this sense, partly a misnomer. It is ironic that someone can be regarded as "out of mind" or ill for the first time in his life just upon emerging from a lifelong deeper ignorance in which those around him were still enshrouded.

Much debate over what paranoia is, like much debate over what schizophrenia is, is really a dispute about how the word should be defined. Possibly, the word ought not to be used at all. If its meaning were taken literally, it might validly apply to certain persons near to the persons to whom it is now applied.

---

* My point here is really tautological. The word "mind," as it is generally used nowadays, is simply the name for a bundle, a collection, a class of all events that are presumed to be "mental." A mental event occurs "in" the mind in the same way that a cat is "in" the class of all cats. It therefore follows necessarily from the definition of mind that an event not thought to be mental does not happen in the mind.

THE CONTEXT, THE BACKGROUND, AND THE LEGACY

1. The Context

Dr. Politzer, speaking about Dr. Schreber, the father, says:

> Every age produces its man who expresses its spirit as if with the power of Providence . . . the generation of our century demanded and created a man like Schreber. (1862, p. 2)

Nearly everyone who has studied families of persons labeled paranoid or schizophrenic agrees that the irrationality of the schizophrenic finds its rationality in the context of his first family. In what context does that family context find its rationality? What is the social *network* around the family of a paranoid or a schizophrenic, and what are its properties? (See Speck, 1966, and Speck and Attneave, 1970.) Where do the patterns of thought, word, and deed of parents of mad offspring fit in? We would be wise, I think, to confess we do not know.

A man renowned as a great pedagogue—Freud said his activities "exerted a lasting influence on his contemporaries"—has two sons. One kills himself and the other goes mad. In what social context can Dr. Schreber's system of child-rearing find its rationality? Why was his system so highly valued?

Schreber, the son, transformed his memory of his father into God. Recall that his sister Anna had linked her memory of God's presence in the Schreber home with her father. She was in step with others' views of her father. Politzer, whose eulogy for him was printed the year after his death in a German *medical* journal, says "our piety for him must be unfading" and compares him to an "emissary of Providence." Freud, writing fifty years after the father's death, says the father "was no insignificant person":

> Such a father as this was by no means unsuitable for transfiguration into a God in the affectionate memory of the son. . . .
> (*Standard Edition, 12,* p. 51)

Freud is surely reflecting a prevailing opinion of Dr. Schreber.

The son had been raised and continued to live in a social context where other people were connecting his father with God. The views of a large network of people may have influenced the operation whereby he substituted God for father. But why did they esteem the father so highly?

Politzer extolled Dr. Schreber as an "observer," a "practical psychologist with the most extensive physiological knowledge," and a "doctor, teacher, dietician, anthropologist, gymnast, and physical therapist." Politzer, after describing what he saw as the "degenerate decadence" of the "age," spiritually and physically, declared

> Such a man had to be created for such an age, and such a man was Schreber. (1862, p. 2)

He said:

> What the German nation and what humanity in general have lost in him has been proclaimed to the world in eloquent words in journals of all persuasions. (*Ibid.,* p. 1)

He thought Dr. Schreber had had "a lasting, fruitful, and epoch-making effect." Dr. Schreber's books, he wrote,

> which went through many editions and translations in almost all languages in a short time, are the most glowing testimonial that his doctrines and methods have been adopted by most people. . . . (p. 5)

Dr. Schreber's *Medical Indoor Gymnastics* has sold nearly forty editions and is translated into seven languages. His behavior has been part of a very large network indeed.

His son says,

> *God did not really understand the living human being.* . . . (*Memoirs*, p. 75; italics in original)

He considers God's

> actions have been practised against me for years with the utmost cruelty and disregard as only a beast deals with its prey. (*Ibid.*, p. 252)

Had he replaced God with father, he would have been telling the plain truth about his childhood experience. But had he told the truth, he might have found no one, while he was alive or for years after his death, to appreciate it.

Much scholarship has been devoted to understanding Schreber; all of it until recently ignored his father's writings as data. Why? Why did those who wrote about Schreber after Freud ignore Freud's neglect of the father's books?

Schreber's father was a key figure in a conspiracy of certain German parents against their children. The conspirators did not see themselves as conspirators. Possibly, they were treating their children as their parents had treated them.

Edwin Lemert (1962), an American sociologist who studied the interpersonal networks around people considered paranoid, found that

> The general idea that the paranoid person symbolically fabricates the conspiracy against him is in our own estimation in-

correct or incomplete. Nor can we agree that he lacks insight, as is so frequently claimed. To the contrary, many paranoid persons properly realise that they are being isolated and excluded by concerted interaction, or that they are being manipulated. However, they are at loss to estimate accurately or realistically the dimensions and form of the coalition arrayed against them. (p. 14)

Schreber was born into a conspiracy against him. Those who tried, while he lived and after he died, to render his experience intelligible failed to see the conspiracy. In failing to see the conspiracy, they sustained it, unwittingly. We need to know how to render *their* failure intelligible.

2. The Background

How had Dr. Schreber, the father, arrived at his views? What sort of people were *his* father and mother, and *their* parents? Who were his teachers? We should like to know more than we can find out. We are not even sure which writers influenced him. Ritter says about him:

> It would be fascinating for the biographer of Schreber to trace his intellectual development in detail. But here all the sources are missing, his study-books are lost, lists of his own or of borrowed books have never been available, and even the . . . University of Leipzig . . . could not provide any information on Schreber's teachers. We are thus left entirely to our own assumptions. (1936, p. 24)

Dr. Schreber's views on raising children and on other matters such as God, history, and the German nation are similar to those of Johann Gottlieb Fichte (1762–1814), the German philosopher and educator. Fichte is considered a philosophical forefather of Nazism. Both he and Dr. Schreber thought the basic aim of education is to attain true religion. I cannot be sure that Dr. Schreber knew his ideas or read his books; it is likely he did, since Fichte's impact upon German thought was strong in the years Dr. Schreber was being educated. Dr Schreber was six years old in the year Fichte died. In discussing Fichte briefly I wish to establish that Dr. Schreber was not alone in his views, but was, as Ritter says, a "child of his time."

Fichte thought "the kingdom of heaven is a theocracy . . . for the blind belief of all"; he says:

> How can such a system be conceived on earth and in the present world and under its laws? That is the question. (1926, p. 273)

> Man is subject to the will of God . . . *without obedience he is nothing and does not really exist at all.* Now this view is that of Christianity or of philosophy which are *synonymous in this connection* [!] The necessary education must, therefore, possess the art of bringing all men without exception infallibly to this view. . . . (*Ibid.*, p. 273)

Fichte here is projecting onto "heaven" an earthly scenario (from his family of origin? his social network? his church?) and adopting that *projection* as an ideal for men to follow. The history of Western political philosophy abounds with similar attempts to justify despotism: they set forth a despotism "above," which is in fact a model of the ones "below," to serve in turn as a model for making the ones below seem lawful.

In his writings on education Fichte outlines how he would improve society. The first thing a child must learn is subjection to someone else. Parents must use "compulsion" on the children such that children have

> freedom only within the sphere in which compulsion ceases, and this freedom is to be regarded as the result of the parents' actions. (p. 129)

Children must have some freedom because without free choice they could not become "moral," another goal for Fichte; he calls the "freedom" the child keeps the child's "voluntary obedience":

> This voluntary obedience consists in the children doing voluntarily, without compulsion and without fear of compulsion, what the parents command, and abstaining voluntarily from what they forbid, because they have forbidden or commanded it. For if the children themselves are convinced of the goodness and appropriateness of what is commanded, and so convinced that their own inclination already prompts them thereto, then this is not obedience but *insight*. (p. 129)

In Fichte's system, as in Dr. Schreber's, freedom means obedience to authority and nothing else; in both systems the child does what his parents want him to do while thinking it is what he wants. Fichte feels the child's view of "goodness" must come from parents. If the child thinks it comes from himself (though it really comes from them), Fichte says he has "insight."

Fichte says "if anything proves that there is good in human nature, it is this obedience": the "childlike trust in the higher wisdom and goodness of parents *generally*"—i.e., no matter how stupid or narrow-minded the parents might be. He likens the "childlike obedience" to the "love or sympathy of the wife." Fichte, like Dr. Schreber, compares a father to God:

> As the educated man conducts himself in relation to the moral law in general and to its executor, God, so the child conducts himself in relation to the commands of his parents. In Christianity God is represented in the image of the Father. This is excellent . . . Let us think . . . of our dutiful obedience to Him and of childlike submission to His will. . . . The development of this obedience is the only means whereby parents can directly produce a moral disposition in the child. . . . (p. 130)

In *Addresses to the German Nation*, a major document of German nationalism, Fichte proposes an

> absolutely new system of German national education, such as has never existed in any other nation. (1922, p. 19)

> The new education must consist essentially in this, that it com-
> pletely destroys freedom of will in the soil which it undertakes
> to cultivate. . . . (*Ibid.*, p. 20)

"If you want to influence" a child,

> you must do more than merely talk to him; you must fashion
> him, and fashion him in such a way that he simply cannot will
> otherwise than you wish him to will. (p. 21)

And who had influenced Fichte? He acknowledges especially
Martin Luther; other nineteenth-century German educators do
also. Fichte says Luther

> became the pattern for all generations to come, and died for us
> all. (p. 7)

Luther had won "freedom," says Fichte, for the "children of
God." Luther had said three centuries earlier:

> There are no better works than to obey and serve all those
> who are set over us as superiors. For this reason also disobedi-
> ence is a greater sin than murder, unchastity, theft, and dis-
> honesty, and all that these may include. (quoted by Sabine,
> 1961, p. 361)

Although many, perhaps most, German educators of the time
would not have disputed these principles, some put forth different views. Friedrich W. A. Froebel (1782–1852), who opened
the first "*Kindergarten*" and gave it this name, wrote in 1826
that in order to bring out the "divine" in children, one had to
leave them "undisturbed"; he opposed "all active, dictatorial,
rigid, and forcibly interfering education and instruction"; he
thought child-rearing should be "passive," not "prescriptive,"
in order to allow children to unfold their powers. (Translated
1885; see pp. 2–14.) My impression is that only a minority of
educators adopted this approach.

Dr. Schreber, the father, spoke for and fostered the climate
of his time. But he was only one pimple of a large rash; most
of his pedagogical colleagues shared his premises.

Ideas similar to Fichte's and Dr. Schreber's were widely held in the nineteenth-century English-speaking world too. Here are two fanciful English pieces of Victorian literature for children:

> Have you not heard what dreadful plagues
> Are threatened by the Lord,
> To him that breaks his father's law
> Or mocks his mother's word?
>
> What heavy guilt upon him lies!
> How cursed is his name!
> The ravens shall pick out his eyes
> And eagles eat the same.
>
> (Isaac Watts,
> *Divine and Moral Songs for Children,* 1715)

No worse sign of a child's character can appear than a readiness to speak lightly of a parent's authority. The great God who made heaven and earth, and can make good all He says, looks upon disobedience to parents as one of the most grievous sins a child can commit, and pronounces a dreadful curse upon it. (Anonymous, *The Children's Friend,* 1868)

Many of the persons who treated or wrote about Schreber, the son, later on, without linking his "nervous illness" to his father's activities, failed to assert a higher or wider rationality against which to measure certain elements in the prevailing one.* They may have been brought up by the same authoritarian, patriarchal principles Schreber's father practiced. Those principles forbade challenges to the system of principles, wishes to challenge them, bitterness at being ruled by them, or even awareness of being ruled by them. Possibly, for them to have acknowledged Schreber's feelings of persecution as valid, in some

---

* Many people posit factors or causes of one sort or another to explain what is regarded as deviance, but think none are needed to understand the acceptance of widely held norms.

sense, might have meant to break rules governing their own minds. Instead, they regarded his protests only as symptoms of a disease process; in so doing they invalidated him. In many of their families Father was probably God too. But they were discreet about it. Schreber was indiscreet.

Theorists of the human mind who lived in this climate and whose views still have influence thought that one's "wish" or "need" to be governed by an external authority derives from one's "drives" or "instincts." I wonder if "drives" or "instincts" would take this form if adults did not persuade and force children to believe they are good to have such wishes and needs and bad not to have them.

Much philosophy, religion, and literature has endorsed blind submission to external power as the greatest good and has condemned disobedience as evil. This may partly explain why many people today think the guilt attached to certain ghastly acts is diminished if done under someone else's orders. Since the West now regards much of what it used to see as evil as evidence of mental illness (see Szasz, 1970, who elaborates this), it may also partly explain why certain parents and teachers think any disobedient child needs psychiatric treatment.

3. The Legacy

The road to renewal of the German essence and the German strength necessarily involves acknowledgement of blood and soil. Only an intimate alliance with the German soil creates the heroic faith in the country of our fathers, the faith which has little regard for one's own benefit, but for the interest of the Nation; an absolutely metaphysical, political faith and will.

It is our duty in this present time—which has awakened to a new life—to remember in gratitude the man who was one of the first men to call upon us to return to the soil of our fathers. Streets and gardens bear his name, but who knows more about him than this? This small paper may show the present era the richness which Schreber's name conceals.

Alfons Ritter, 1936, p. 3

Dr. Schreber wanted his child-rearing system to have enduring macro-social effects. He dedicated his *Kallipädie* (1858), from which I have quoted much, "to the salvation of future generations."

He urged "governments" to "take in hand" children's training "in a much more serious way than has happened heretofore" (*ibid.*, p. 25). He titled three of his books *Gymnastics from a Medical Viewpoint Represented Also as a Concern for the State* (1843), *Concerning the Education of the Nation and its Up-to-date Development, by Elevating the Teaching Profession and by the Bringing Together of School and Home* (1860), and *The Friend of the Family as Pedagogue and Guide [Führer] to Family Happiness, National Health, and Cultivation of Human Beings: for Fathers and Mothers of the German Nation* (1861a). He said

Alongside the education of the person, one must take the direction of educating a future citizen. (1858, p. 165)

In 1843 he approached the Assembly of the Diet of the Kingdom of Saxony to ask for the general introduction of gymnastics by the state. He said in so doing he saw himself as "the humble organ of a general voice," as representing many people's "vivid longing" (Ritter, 1936, pp. 18–19).

He wanted the state to ensure, for the sake of "the preservation of the clear mind of youth," "the most complete severity of school activity and *severity of discipline*"; he favored "a modified *military strictness*" at all schools to keep "the noble zestful mind best in full swing" (1860, p. 36).

He thought governments must aim for their citizens, like parents for their children,

towards the ideal of creation which is implicit in human nature, towards the outright conception [*Urbilde*] of man planned and desired by God; . . . to an ever better realisation of the divine plan of human creation, as this plan is revealed both by philosophy and the spirit of universal history as well as by the spirit of Christianity. . . . (*Ibid.*, p. 4)

He asserts here divine, philosophical, historical, and Christian authority for his and his colleagues' parochial, ethnocentric views of education which he wishes to see governments enforce.

He says it is the responsibility of the physician, more than of the politician or philosopher,

> to investigate the conditions of nature in which the life and well-being of the human (physical-spiritual) organism is based, both the individual organism and the *organism of the state*. . . . (p. 3)

His national state, like Thomas Hobbes' Leviathan, is an "organism" to be governed by *"natural laws."* Dr. Schreber, by applying the biological *analogy* (MacMurray, 1957, and Laing and Esterson, 1964) to the state, tries to annex by a sort of medical imperialism the province of national politics for the domain of medicine and for himself. He believes, falsely, that medicine has scientific knowledge about the well-being of the state. To see the state or any group of people as a biological unit adds nothing to our knowledge of biology or groups of people.

John MacMurray, the English philosopher, might be right to say flatly

> So long as our most adequate concept is the organic concept, our social planning can only issue in a totalitarian society. (1957, p. 83)

Dr. Schreber saw people who did not match his moral ideals as ill or *as illnesses*. He regarded the "lower classes," if they were not educated toward "ennoblement of life in accordance with reason, with nature, and by moral power," as *"tumours on the body of the state"* (1860, p. 14). He regarded elements in the state that are "unviable," "rotten," and "injurious" as *"unhealthy"* and as "weeds"—they can "find no nourishment" where the "heart of the state is healthy."

The idea that persons or groups of persons *are* illnesses is nonsensical, though dangerous, if widely held. Dr. Schreber's views are precursors of those of the Nazis eighty years later, who killed people for the sake of the "hygiene" and "health" of the "race."

Politzer, Dr. Schreber's contemporary, says:

> Subsequent generations will harvest what he has sown, people who are related to him in mind and spirit will continue to work the ground he has prepared and levelled. (1862, p. 4)

> If every country had many such men as Schreber, mankind would not have to worry about its future. (*Ibid.*, p. 7)

Remember: Hitler and his peers were raised when Dr. Schreber's books, preaching household totalitarianism, were popular.

I am not alone in intuiting a possible link between microsocial despotism in the Schreber family and the macro-social despotism of Nazi Germany. Elias Canetti, a novelist and sociologist, also did in his discussion (1962) of paranoia and power. He does not mention Schreber's father; he thinks of the link with Nazism, using only the *Memoirs* as data. He states about the *son's* view of God's system of power:

> We shall find in Schreber a *political* system of a disturbingly familiar kind. (1962, p. 443)

He says Schreber, the son, gives us

> a very distinct picture of God: he is a despot and nothing else. His realm contains provinces and factions. "God's interests," as they are bluntly and summarily designated, demand the increase of his power. . . ; human beings who hinder him are done away with. It cannot be denied that this is a God who sits in the web of his policy like a spider. (*Ibid.*, p. 444)

Again referring to the son's "revelations," Canetti says:

> As no-one today is likely to deny, his [Schreber's, the son's] political system had within a few decades been accorded high honour: though in a rather cruder and less literate form it became the creed of a great nation, leading . . . to the conquest of Europe and coming within a hair's breadth of the conquest of the world. Thus Schreber's claims were posthumously vindicated by his unwitting disciples. We are not likely to accord him the same recognition, but the amazing and incontrovertible likeness between the two systems may serve to justify the time we have devoted to this single case of paranoia. . . .
> (p. 447)

Ritter, writing about Dr. Schreber, the father, in 1936, saw in him a spiritual precursor of Nazism. Ritter admired both Dr. Schreber and Hitler.

Anyone who wishes to understand German "character structure" in the Nazi era could profitably study Dr. Schreber's books.

There are many passages in Hitler's *Mein Kampf* (1939) that resemble Dr. Schreber's views. Hitler, like Dr. Schreber, abhors what he calls weakness, cowardice, laziness, softness, and indolence. He speaks, as Dr. Schreber does, of the "moral and physical decadence" of his time (p. 352).

Hitler, like Dr. Schreber, demands compliance with parts of his *own* mind he calls the Divine Will and Nature; Nature, for Hitler, is the "ruthless Queen of Wisdom" (p. 124). Hitler condemns pre-Nazi society for committing sins "against the image of God" (p. 352). Hitler and Dr. Schreber urge obedience to what they must experience as overwhelming powers: "God," "Fate," "Necessity," and "History." These indeterminate abstractions are, in fact, names for programs governing *their* minds. Hitler and Dr. Schreber, in pretending to derive from them authority over others, are also submitting to them themselves. The control they impose upon others is the control that controls themselves.

Hitler's attitude toward the "masses" is similar to Dr. Schreber's implied feelings toward children, but much more cynical:

> The *psyche* of the broad masses is accessible only to what is strong and uncompromising. Like a woman whose inner sensibilities are not so much under the sway of abstract reasoning but are always subject to the influence of a vague emotional longing for the strength that completes her being, and who would rather bow to the strong man. . . . —in like manner the masses of the people prefer the ruler to the suppliant and are filled with a stronger sense of mental security by a teaching that brooks no rival than by a teaching which offers them a liberal choice. They have very little idea of how to make such a choice, and thus they are prone to feel that they have been abandoned. They feel very little shame at being terrorized intellectually and they are scarcely conscious of the fact that their freedom as human beings is impudently abused; and thus they have not the slightest suspicion of the intrinsic fallacy of the whole doctrine. They see only the ruthless force and brutality of its determined utterances, to which they always submit. (1939, p. 47)

Wilhelm Reich does not discuss Schreber, the son, as far as I know and never mentions Schreber's father. But he gets the point perfectly. In *The Mass Psychology of Fascism* he says:

> The father's economic position as well as his position in the state are reflected in his patriarchal relationship with the other members of his family. The authoritarian state has a representative in every family, the father; in this way he becomes the state's most valuable tool.
>
> The father's authoritarian position reflects his political role and discloses the relationship of family and authoritarian state. The same position which the boss holds in the production process, the father maintains in the family. He in turn produces submissiveness to authority in his children, especially his sons. This is the basis of the passive, submissive attitude of middle class individuals towards Führer figures. Without really knowing it, Hitler built upon this attitude of the lower middle classes.
>
> The people in their overwhelming majority are so femi-

> nine by nature and attitude that sober reasoning determines
> their thoughts and actions far less than emotion and feel-
> ing . . ." MEIN KAMPF
> It is not a matter of being that way "by nature" but of being a
> typical example of the reproduction of an authoritarian social
> system in the structures of its members. (1946, pp. 44–45)

Of course. Despotism at any level—state, factory, school, church, family, individual—breeds and needs despotism at all levels.

Later Reich writes:

> German fascism was born from the biological rigidity and
> crippling of the former generation. Prussian militarism, with its
> machine-like discipline, its goose-step, its "belly in, chest out!"
> is the extreme manifestation of this biological rigidity . . . It is
> clear: social freedom and self-regulation are inconceivable in
> rigid, machine-like people. (*Ibid.*, p. 301)

Dr. Schreber's exercises in obedience and stiff posture had given some Prussian soldiers their basic training from infancy.

Hitler talks of training children in erect posture:

> In the People's State the army will no longer be obliged to
> teach boys how to walk and stand erect. . . . (1939, p. 358)

The army will no longer need to because families and especially schools will already have done the job.

A cost of training soldiers from babyhood may be that some babies go mad later on. A good or a bad bargain according to one's values.

EPILOGUE

Totalitarian societies from Sparta to Soviet Russia have practiced principles of child-rearing that Dr. Schreber preached—especially the emphasis on obedience and discipline. Dr. Schreber would have endorsed many of their attitudes. Consider an authoritative Russian manual, *Parents and Children*, prepared by the Academy of Pedagogical Sciences and published in 1961. Its aim is

> helping parents to bring up their children properly so that they can grow up to be worthy citizens of our socialist nation. (quoted by Bronfenbrenner, 1970, pp. 9–10)

In a chapter on discipline it says:

> The child must fulfill requests that adults make of him—this is the first thing the child must be taught. The child must fulfill the demands of his elders. (*Ibid.*, p. 10)

A popular Russian work on child-rearing says:

> Obedience in adolescents and older school children—this is the effective expression of their love, trust, and respect towards parents and other adult family members, a conscious desire to acknowledge their experience and wisdom. This is an important aspect of preparing young people for life in a Communist society. (*Ibid.*, pp. 10–11)

175

But to obey is not enough; the child must also develop self-discipline:

> It is necessary as early as possible to develop in the young child an active, positive relation to the demands of adults, the desire to act in accordance with these demands, to do that which is necessary. Herein lies the great significance of our efforts in developing conscious self-discipline, indeed its very elements. Every person, including the young school-age child, will better, more quickly, and more joyously fulfill demands and rules once he has a desire to do so. (p. 10)

Russian schools aim at character education *(vospitanie);* their goal is to develop "Communist morality" (p. 26). Official Russian views on child-rearing mirror in spirit some of Dr. Schreber's ideas over a hundred years ago though they are less confusing than his; he called obedience freedom. He also would have substituted the word "Christian" for "Communist."

Upbringing in Russia does not succeed with everyone. Soviet psychiatrists today treat as ill certain adults who lack "a conscious desire to acknowledge" the "experience and wisdom" of the Russian rulers. The psychiatrists consider what they call reformist ideas a symptom of mental illness. They see many people with such a "symptom" as paranoid, i.e., as imagining they are persecuted when they really are not, and treat them accordingly. The psychiatrists' behavior could *induce* or aggravate feelings of persecution in their so-called paranoid patients. If the "patients" see as persecution what the psychiatrists see as therapy, and if the psychiatrists see the "patients' " view as proving they need therapy, a very vicious spiral is on. We in the West see those psychiatrists as petty bureaucrats acting as if on behalf of an invisible Ministry of Social Adjustment. Probably many of the psychiatrists do not see their behavior as persecution although not all may be naïve.

In the Utopia of B. F. Skinner, the Harvard psychologist (1962 and 1971), control of human beings from childhood would be so "scientific" that dissidence with the established order would not occur:

> We can achieve a sort of control under which the controlled, though they are following a code much more scrupulously than was ever the case under the old system nevertheless feel free. They are doing what they want to do, not what they are forced to do. That's the source of the tremendous power of positive reinforcement—there's no restraint and no revolt. By a careful cultural design, we control not the final behaviour, but the inclination to behave—the motives, the desires, the wishes.
>
> The curious thing is that in that case the question of freedom never arises. (1962, p. 262)

Recently, Skinner's views have received much publicity. Like Dr. Schreber and the Russians, Skinner wishes to improve society by programming children to experience and act in certain ways. He calls the means he would adopt conditioning or positive reinforcement; Dr. Schreber called his means habituation. Like Dr. Schreber, he cloaks his ideas about man, mind, and society in scientific rhetoric but offers little *relevant* scientific evidence to support them; no scientific evidence to support his *aims* exists.

Skinner might think he knows enough in order to start creating better persons and cultures; so did Dr. Schreber. Dr. Schreber was sure his system would *prevent* mental illness. Remember the reverence which society, including physicians, accorded him.

Who can vouch for the "experts"? Suppose the scientific technology to "design" (Skinner's term) children existed, which it does not: what if the "designers" were designed themselves in such ways that their designing of children confused children and drove them mad? What if those children who might otherwise grow up to become enlightened social critics, would be especially likely to be driven mad? Certain children might see as persecution what the "experts" see as "positive reinforcement" or "love."

It has been a thesis of this book that people considered paranoid experience as persecution what people around them experience differently. Feelings of persecution are no less prevalent in Western society than anywhere else, as far as I know. Therefore, you would be mistaken to think what I have been saying applies only to Them—Dr. Schreber's Germany, the Nazis, Soviet Russia, or Skinner's "Utopia"—and not to Us.

I propose an experiment:

> Presume in all cases of "paranoia," in which no intoxication or organic disease is present, that the person who feels persecuted is responding to behavior, past or present, of other people who are or have been near him.

> Starting from this point, invite everyone in his social situation to search for the origin of his feelings of persecution.

I suggest that this sort of shift of focus would enlighten, though it might also frighten, all concerned. It could bring into view and into question some secret premises about "normal" family life that most people share, and constraints they also share against seeing or questioning those premises.

The issues I have discussed in this book touch upon much that is the matter with certain macro-social and micro-social human systems. Maybe nothing can be done about it. Psychologies and psychiatries, East and West, support and administer the existing state of affairs; it is easier for West to see East doing it than to see itself doing it. If psychologies and psychiatries do not bring the status quo into question, can anyone? I do not know; perhaps we, you and I, laymen and professionals, *are* the answers.

A dictum some people attribute to Confucius says:

> If you wish to set your kingdom right, first set your province right; to set your province right, first set your city right; to set your city right, first set your clan right; to set your clan right, first set your family right; and to set your family right, first set yourself right; then— . . .

178

BIBLIOGRAPHY

Besides the references noted in the text, a few more that are directly relevant to this book are included.

ANONYMOUS (1868). *The Children's Friend,* London: Seeley & Co., quoted in Temple, N., *Seen and Not Heard: A Garland of Fancies for Victorian Children,* London: Hutchinson, 1970.

ASHBY, R. A. (1956). *An Introduction to Cybernetics,* London: Chapman & Hall.

BATESON, G., JACKSON, D. D., HALEY, J., and WEAKLAND, J. (1956). "Toward a Theory of Schizophrenia," *Behavioural Science,* 1: 251–264.

BAUMEYER, F. (1956). "The Schreber Case," *International J. Psychoanal.,* 37: 61–74.

——————— (1970). *"Noch ein Nachtrag zu Freuds Arbeit über Schreber,"* Zeitschrift für Psychosomatische Medizin und Psychoanalyse, 16: 243 245.

BIRDWHISTELL, R. (1970). *Kinesics and Context, Essays on Body Motion Communication,* Philadelphia: University of Pennsylvania Press.

BLEULER, E. (1924). *Textbook of Psychiatry,* Authorized English Edition by A. A. Brill, New York: Macmillan.

——————— (1950). *Dementia Praecox or The Group of Schizophrenias,* translated by J. Zinkin, New York: International Universities Press.

BLOCH, I. (1908). *The Sexual Life of our Time,* translated from the 6th German edition by Paul, M. E., London: Rebman; cited by Hare, E. H. (see below).

BRONFENBRENNER, U. (1970). *Two Worlds of Childhood, U.S. and U.S.S.R.*, New York: Russell Sage Foundation.

CANETTI, E. (1962). *Crowds and Power*, London: Gollancz Ltd., translated by C. Stewart from *Masse und Macht*, Hamburg: Claasen Verlag, 1960.

COMFORT, A. (1967). *The Anxiety Makers*, London: Thomas Nelson & Sons.

DEVEREUX, G. (1953). "Why Oedipus Killed Laius, A Note on the Complementary Oedipus Complex in Greek Drama," *International J. Psychoanal.*, 34: 132–141.

VON DOMARUS, E. (1964). "The Specific Laws of Logic in Schizophrenia" in *Language and Thought in Schizophrenia*, edited by Kasanin, J. S., New York: W. W. Norton & Co.

DUFFY, J. (1963). "Masturbation and Clitoridectomy, A Nineteenth-Century View," *J. Amer. Medical Assoc.*, 186: No. 3, 246–248.

ELIADE, M. (1960). *Myths, Dreams, and Mysteries*, translated by P. Mairet, Great Britain: Harvill Press.

——————— (1964). *Shamanism, Archaic Techniques of Ecstasy*, translated by Trask, W. R., New York: Bollingen Foundation.

ESTERSON, A. (1970). *The Leaves of Spring*, London: Tavistock.

EVANS-WENTZ, W. Y. (1927). *The Tibetan Book of the Dead*, London: Oxford University Press.

——————— (1969). *Tibet's Great Yogi Milarepa*, London: Oxford University Press, paperback edition.

FAIRBAIRN, W. R. D. (1956). "Considerations Arising out of the Schreber Case," *British J. of Med. Psychology*, 29, Part 2: 113–137.

FICHTE, J. G. (1922). *Addresses to the German Nation*, translated by Jones, R. F. and Turnbull, G. H., Chicago and London: The Open Court Publishing Co.

——————— (1926). *The Educational Theory of J. G. Fichte*, translated and edited by Turnbull, G. H., London: University Press of Liverpool and Hodder and Stoughton.

FLECHSIG, P. E. (1884). "Für gynaekologischen Behandlung der Hysterie," *Neurologisches Centralblatt*, 3, 19: 433–439 and 20: 457–468.

FOUCAULT, M. (1970). *The Order of Things, An Archaeology of the*

Human Sciences, London: Tavistock, translated from *Les Mots et les Choses*.

FREUD, S. (1963). *The Standard Edition of the Complete Psychological Works of Sigmund Freud*, London: The Hogarth Press and the Institute of Psycho-analysis.

FROEBEL, F. (1885). *Education of Man*, translated by Josephine Jarvis, New York: A. Lovell & Co.

FROMM, E., NARVÁEZ, F. and others (1968). "The Oedipus Complex: Comments on 'The Case of Little Hans,'" *Contemporary Psychoanalysis*, Vol. 4, No. 2: 178-188.

GRAVES, R. (1960). *The Greek Myths* (in two volumes), England: Penguin Books.

GRODDECK, G. (1951). *The Unknown Self*, London: Vision Press.

———— (1961). *The Book of the It*, New York: The New American Library of World Literature, Mentor Books.

GROF, S. (1970). "Beyond Psychoanalysis I: The Implications of LSD Research For Understanding Dimensions of Human Personality" *Darshana International*, Vol. 10, No. 3.

HALEY, J. (1963). *Strategies of Psychotherapy*, New York: Grune & Stratton.

HARE, E. H. (1962). "Masturbatory Insanity: The History of an Idea," *J. of Mental Science*, 108: 1-25.

HIGGINS, M. and RAPHAEL, C. M., editors, (1968). *Reich Speaks of Freud*, New York: Noonday Press, a division of Farrar, Straus & Giroux.

HITLER, A. (1939). *Mein Kampf*, translated by Murphy, J., London: Hutchinson & Co. in association with Hurst & Blackett.

HOFFMAN, H. (1845). *Struwwelpeter*. The English *Struwwelpeter*, 1890, London: Routledge, Kegan & Paul Ltd.

JUNG, C. G. (1962). *Symbols of Transformation*, New York: Harper Torchbooks.

KLEIN, M. (1948). *Contributions to Psycho-analysis*, London: Hogarth Press.

KNIGHT, R. P. (1940). "The Relationship of Latent Homosexuality to the Mechanism of Paranoid Delusions," *Bull. Menninger Clinic*, 4: 149-159.

KRAEPELIN, E. (1904). *Lectures on Clinical Psychiatry*, revised and edited by Johnstone, T., London: Baillière, Tindall, and Cox.

KUHN, T. S. (1970). *The Structure of Scientific Revolutions,* 2nd Edition, Chicago: The University of Chicago Press.

LACAN, J. (1957). *"L'instance de la lettre dans l'inconscient ou la raison depuis Freud,"* La Psychanalyse III: 47–81. Translated as "The Insistence of the Letter in the Unconscious," in Ehrmann, J., editor (1970), *Structuralism,* New York: Anchor Books.

LAING, R. D. (1965). "Mystification, Confusion, and Conflict" in *Intensive Family Therapy,* edited by Boszormenyi-Nagy, I. and Framo, J. L. New York: Hoeber Medical Division, Harper & Row.

————— (1971). *The Politics of the Family and Other Essays,* London: Tavistock.

————— and ESTERSON, A. (1964). *Sanity, Madness and the Family,* London: Tavistock Publications.

LEMERT, E. M. (1962). "Paranoia and the Dynamics of Exclusion," *Sociometry,* 25: 2–20.

LILLY, J. C. (1970). "Programming and Metaprogramming in the Human Biocomputer: Theory and Experiments," Menlo Park, California: Whole Earth Catalog and Berkeley, California: Book People.

MACALPINE, I. and HUNTER, R. A. See SCHREBER, D. P.

MACMURRAY, J. (1957). *The Self as Agent.* London: Faber and Faber.

MASTERS, R. E. L., editor (1967). *Sexual Self-Stimulation,* Los Angeles: Sherbourne Press.

MENNINGER, K. (1942). *Love Against Hate,* New York: Harcourt Brace.

MOWRER, O. H. (1953). *Psychotherapy Theory and Research,* New York: Ronald.

NIEDERLAND, W. G. (1959a). "The 'Miracled-Up' World of Schreber's Childhood," *Psychoanal. Stud. Child,* 14: 383–413.

————— (1959b). "Schreber: Father and Son," *Psychoanal. Quarterly,* 28: 151–169.

————— (1960). "Schreber's Father," *J. Am. Psychoanal. Assn.,* 8: 492–499.

————— (1963). "Further Data and Memorabilia Pertaining to the Schreber Case," *Int. J. Psychoanal.,* 44: 201–207.

POLITZER, L. M. (1862). "Daniel Gottlieb Moritz Schreber," *Jahrbuch für Kinderheilkunde und Physische Erziehung*, Vol. 5, No. 2: 1–7.

RANK, O. (1912). *Das Inzestmotiv in Dichtungund Sage*, Leipzig: Deuticke.

———— (1952). *The Trauma of Birth*, New York: Robert Brunner.

REICH, W. (1946). *The Mass Psychology of Fascism*, U.S.A.: The Albion Press (Limited Edition); also New York: Farrar, Straus & Giroux, 1971.

RITTER, A. (1936). *Schreber, das Bildungssystem eines Arztes*, Inaugural Dissertation, Erlangen University.

RUSSELL, B. (1961). *Religion and Science*, London and New York: Oxford.

SABINE, G. H. (1961). *A History of Political Theory*, Third Edition, London: Holt, Rinehart and Winston.

SCHATZMAN, M. (1970). "Madness and Morals" in *Counter Culture*, edited by Berke, J., London: Peter Owen. Reprinted in *The Radical Therapist*, edited by Agel, J., New York: Ballantine Books, 1971, and in *R. D. Laing and Anti-Psychiatry*, edited by Boyers, R., New York: Perennial Library, Harper & Row, 1971.

———— (1971). "Paranoia and Persecution: The Case of Schreber," *Family Process*, 10, 2: 177–207.

SCHREBER, D. G. M. (1839). *Das Buch der Gesundheit* (The Book of Health), Leipzig: H. Fries.

———— (1842). *Die Kaltwasserheilmethode* (The Cold-Water Healing Method), name of publisher unavailable.

———— (1843). *Das Turnen vom ärztlichen Standpunkte aus, zugleich als eine Staatsangelegenheit dargestellt* (Gymnastics from a Medical Viewpoint Represented Also as a Concern for the State), name of publisher unavailable.

———— (1852). *Die Eigentümlichkeiten des kindlichen Organismus* (The Characteristics of the Child's Organism), Leipzig: Fleischer.

———— (1853). *Die schädlichen Körperhaltungen und Gewohnheiten der Kinder nebst Angabe der Mittel dagegen* (The Harmful Body Positions and Habits of Children, Including a Statement of Counteracting Measures), Leipzig: Fleischer.

———— (1858). *Kallipädie oder Erziehung zur Schönheit durch naturgetreue und gleichmässige Förderung normaler*

Körperbildung (Education Toward Beauty by Natural and Balanced Furtherance of Normal Body Growth), Leipzig: Fleischer.

——————— (1859). *Die planmässige Schärfung der Sinnesorgane* (The Systematically Planned Sharpening of the Sense Organs), Leipzig: Fleischer.

——————— (1860). *Über Volkserziehung und zeitgemässe Entwicklung derselben durch Hebung des Lehrerstandes und durch Annäherung von Schule und Haus* (Concerning the Education of the Nation and its Up-to-date Development by Elevating the Teaching Profession and by the Bringing Together of School and Home), Leipzig: Fleischer.

——————— (1861a). *Der Hausfreund als Erzieher und Führer zu Familienglück, Volksgesundheit und Menschenveredlung für Väter und Mütter des deutschen Volkes* (The Friend of the Family as Pedagogue and Guide to Family Happiness, National Health, and Cultivation of Human Beings for Fathers and Mothers of the German Nation), name of publisher unavailable.

——————— (1861b). *Das Buch der Gesundheit oder die Lebenskunst nach der Einrichtung und den Gesetzen der menschlichen Natur* (The Book of Health of the Art of Living according to the Arrangement and the Rules of Human Nature), 2nd Edition, Leipzig: Herman Fries.

——————— (1862). *Das Pangymnastikon* (The Pangymnastikon), Leipzig: Fleischer.

——————— (1899). *Medical Indoor Gymnastics*, 26th edition, Leipzig: Fleischer and London: Williams and Norgate.

SCHREBER, D. P. (1903). *Denkwürdigkeiten eines Nervenkranken*, Leipzig: Oswald, Mutze. Translated and edited by Macalpine, I. and Hunter, R. A., *Memoirs of My Nervous Illness*, London: Dawson & Son, Ltd., 1955.

SEARLES, H. F. (1958). "The Schizophrenic's Vulnerability to the Therapist's Unconscious Processes," *J. Nervous & Mental Dis.*, 127: 247. Reprinted in Searles, H. F. (1965), *Collected Papers on Schizophrenia and Other Subjects*, London: The Hogarth Press and the Institute of Psycho-analysis.

SIIRALA, M. (1961). *Die Schizophrenie des Einzelnen und der All-*

gemeinheit (The Schizophrenia of the Individual and of the Community), Göttingen: Vandenhoek & Ruprecht.

SKINNER, B. F. (1962). *Walden Two,* New York: Macmillan Paperbacks.

———— (1971). *Beyond Freedom and Dignity,* New York: Knopf.

SPECK, R. V. (1966). "Psychotherapy of the Social Network of a Schizophrenic Family," paper presented at the Amer. Psychol. Assoc. Symposium on "Conjoint Family Therapy and Assessment," New York, N.Y., 6 Sept. 1966.

———— and ATTNEAVE, C. L. (1970). "Social Network Intervention" in *Changing Families,* edited by Haley, J., Philadelphia: Grune & Stratton.

SPITZ, R. A. (1953). "Authority and Masturbation," *Yearbook of Psychoanalysis,* 9: 113–145, New York: International Universities Press.

SZASZ, T. (1961). *The Myth of Mental Illness: Foundation of a Theory of Personal Conduct,* New York: Dell, by arrangement with Harper & Row.

———— (1968). "Hysteria" in *International Encyclopedia of the Social Sciences,* U.S.A.: Crowell Collier and Macmillan.

———— (1970). *The Manufacture of Madness,* New York and London: Harper & Row.

WAELDER, R. (1951). "The Structure of Paranoid Ideas," *International J. of Psychoanal.,* 32: 167–177.

WATTS, I. (1715). *Divine and Moral Songs for Children,* London: Religious Tract Society.

WHORF, B. L. (1964). *Language, Thought, and Reality,* edited by Carroll, J. B., Cambridge, Mass.: M.I.T. Press.

WIENER, H. (1966). "External Chemical Messengers: I, Emission and Reception in Man," *N.Y. State J. of Medicine,* 66, 24: 3153–3170.

———— (1967). "External Chemical Messengers: II, Natural History of Schizophrenia," *N.Y. State J. of Medicine,* 67, 9: 1144–1165.

WILDEN, A. (1968). *The Language of the Self: The Function of Language in Psychoanalysis by Jacques Lacan,* Baltimore: Johns Hopkins.

185

WINNICOTT, D. W. (1958). *Collected Papers: Through Paediatrics to Psycho-Analysis*, London: Tavistock.

WITKIN, H. A. and LEWIS, H. B. (1967). "Presleep Experiences and Dreams" in *Experimental Studies of Dreaming*, edited by Witkin and Lewis, New York: Random House.

YAP, P. M. (1965). "Koro—a Culture-Bound Depersonalization Syndrome," *British J. Psych.*, 111: 43–49.

INDEX

ABOUT THE AUTHOR

MORTON SCHATZMAN is an American psychiatrist. He is a graduate of Columbia College and the Albert Einstein College of Medicine and received his psychiatric training at Mt. Sinai and Montefiore hospitals in New York. At the end of his psychiatric training he went to London to work with R. D. Laing and the Philadelphia Association. He is in private practice in London, doing individual, marital, and family psychotherapy.

In 1970 Dr. Schatzman founded the Arbours Housing Association, of which he is Chairman; this is a charity set up to provide help and places to live for people in emotional distress, without seeing, labeling, or treating them as mentally ill. He lives in one such household himself.

Among his interests now are spiritual and psychotic experiences as sources of knowledge about the human mind.

DATE DUE